About the Author

Dr. Kenneth Taylor (b. 1944) was able to explore the USA during leave from his career in the Royal Navy.
He spent time on a ranch in Colorado and visited an Indian Reservation, and has since visited America frequently, validating facts about the history of the West.

Dr. Kenneth's interest in Western History was inspired by watching cowboy films from an early age. This prompted him to search for the true facts over the next five decades.
He has studied in the Daughters of the Republic of Texas Research Library in San Antonio and the University of Texas.

I dedicate this book to my wonderful wife BERYL who is my inspiration for everything I do in life.

Ken Taylor

THE HISTORY OF THE AMERICAN WEST: THE FACTS

A CIP catalogue record for this title is available from the British Library.

ISBN 978 178455 962 5 (Paperback)
ISBN 978 1 78455 964 9 (Hardback)

www.austinmacauley.com

First Published (2015)
Austin Macauley Publishers Ltd.
25 Canada Square
Canary Wharf
London
E14 5LB

Printed and bound in Great Britain

Acknowledgments

I wish to record my grateful thanks to Mike James for his help with the text of my book. Also many thanks to Ron Bygrave and Ian Pearson for applying their computer skills on my behalf. I wish to thank the editorial staff at Austin Macauley for all the help, advice and guidance they have provided.

Contents

Introduction

The American West is a vast landscape of mountain ranges, hills, rivers, canyons and plains. Long before the first Europeans arrived the Native Americans lived off this land, those same natives who would later be incorrectly labelled 'Indians' due to the ignorance of the early white explorers. They hunted the buffalo that roamed free across the immense openness of the continent, continuing a way of life that had been all but unchanged across millennia. To them alone was the splendour of that wild nature, of the snow-capped peaks and the majestic Grand Canyon where the Colorado River flows unceasingly below. They knew the burning heat of mid-day and the icy cold of night, the way that the colours of the rocks gleam in the light of both the sun and the moon, the wonders beyond wonder to which no camera can give justice.

The first Europeans believed that they had reached a land of dreams, a place of unlimited gold, and when the natives were found to have little of value they were usually treated with extreme savagery. However, a greater threat to their way of life occurred when gold was discovered in locations across the continent, as it caused a huge influx of settlers looking to 'get rich quick' and turned those same canyons and plains into a battle ground. The fledgling United States was happy to make deals with the natives, but not so keen to keep those deals once it had guaranteed the rights of its citizens to prospect for gold. The more that settlements and towns grew up on what was originally Native land, and the more treaties that were solemnly signed and then easily cast aside, the more the tension and warfare naturally increased. The Natives had no western style legal documents to 'prove' their ownership of the land, but in reality this made little difference as it was money that was speaking rather than humanity.

Now, many years later, we have cities and skyscrapers instead of towns and shacks. The train and motorcar have replaced the covered wagon, and the freeways link people together in countless miles of freedom that pulsate from state to state.

The American West of yesteryear, the mountains and plains and the life and death in a single moment are still there, the same boiling sun and freezing cold still unchanged, hidden only by our own perception of time and variance. Still, across this teeming country with millions of citizens we look back; we look back and see the real Old West, the true country of hard and rugged people, and we see beyond Hollywood and into the real lives of the men and women who lived and died there.

Native Americans

The indigenous people of North America, Native Americans are composed of numerous tribes, nations and ethnic groupings. They were originally known as 'Indians', after early European explorers were convinced that they had discovered a sea route to India, and the name stuck. The term can now be considered politically incorrect, although many natives still refer to themselves as Indians. Since the beginning of the early-modern era there has been a great deal of conflict between natives and settlers, stretching right up till the end of the nineteenth century. As a result, these battles and skirmishes have a key place in any description of the Old West.

Before European encroachment many Natives lived in hunter-gatherer societies, though in quite a number of groups there was cultivation of crops: most often maize, beans and squash. This was a very different way of life than that which the white settlers brought with them, being a totally agricultural and, in later years, industrial based society. These differences helped to fuel conflicts and made it more difficult for the opposing sides to see eye to eye.

The first contact with native tribes was often established by fur traders who would push into unexplored lands. These tended to have friendly relations with the Indians, as they presented no threat to their way of life. As the United States began to expand its borders and move further west, settlers and miners came into increasing conflict with the tribes of the Great Plains. These were largely nomadic cultures, using horses and travelling to hunt bison. In the years following the Civil War, which was also the golden age of the Old West, these groups fought fiercely against incursions into their lands and the result of this was a series of Indian wars which lasted until around 1890. The development of transcontinental railways increased the pressure on the western tribes and meant that their days as independent nations were numbered; suddenly the ease of cross country transport meant that even formerly isolated areas were opened up to white expansion. The US government began forcing treaties and land cessions on the Indians, frequently breaking agreements and gradually moving them onto specially created reservations. The major idea was that they would try and 'westernise' the natives by showing them how to settle down to farming. However, most of the land that was set aside for reservations was of very poor quality, meaning that farming was not an easy way to survive.

In general, the Native Americans were usually thought of as being somehow sub-human and therefore were treated very badly. This led to terrible crimes being committed by both sides as Indians and whites carried out attacks and reprisal strikes against one another. The US had always made it an aim to eventually expand all the way to the west coast, and this naturally brought about conflict with all the groups who lived within this area.

In films and literature, Indians are normally portrayed in an extremely polarised manner, as being either evil savages who live only to kill, or as saintly beings that existed in complete harmony with nature before the coming of the whites. In fact, the truth is somewhere in the middle, for just like any other human being they were capable of both good and evil. Before the arrival of the Europeans there were wars between different tribes and nations, and atrocities were committed. On the other hand, the classic image of the redskin savage is not correct either. Native culture was extremely complex, certainly as much so as that of the Europeans, with a wide variety of social, religious and political institutions. They were not uncivilised, but rather civilised in a different way.

It would take a huge series of books to do justice to the culture and way of life of Native Americans. For the purposes of understanding their place in the Old West it is enough to say that they were usually viewed with a mixture of fear and contempt by the whites, born out of a complete misunderstanding and lack of respect between the two sides. The desire of the United States to push on to the Pacific Ocean meant that warfare was inevitable, and resulted in a huge amount of misery and death.

Daniel Boone

One of the early frontiersmen, Daniel Boone (1734-1820) was also an explorer and pioneer who became something of a folk hero both in his own time and after. He is best known for exploring and settling modern day Kentucky, and for utilising the 'Cumberland Gap' which is a route through the Appalachian Mountains.

Born to Quaker parents, Boone grew up in western Pennsylvania in a region which was also roamed by Native Americans. Owing to the pacifistic leanings of the Quakers there were few tensions between them and the Indians, though as time passed many native tribes began to slowly move west as the white man encroached further on their former hunting grounds. Boone's father was eventually expelled by the Society of Friends after several of his children married outside of the organisation, though his mother continued to attend their meetings and usually brought the children with her. In general, Daniel Boone had little education, though he learnt to read and was often seen with a book. He also practiced his skills at marksmanship and became a good shot with a rifle.

In the mid-1750s Boone served time in the British army during the French and Indian War, which saw Britain and France fighting over land. Later he served time as a wagon driver, before returning home to marry Rebecca Bryan with whom he eventually had ten children. Following Indian raids, the family relocated to Virginia, and Boone served more time in the army as well as making long distance hunting trips. With a growing family to feed, he was able to supplement his income by selling game that he shot, hunting deer in the autumn and beaver and otter in the winter.

By 1760 the tension with the Native Americans had calmed down and the family were able to return to their old home. Nonetheless, Daniel felt that the area was becoming too crowded and wanted to strike out for the frontier, where there would be more land. At this point in his life he was struggling to pay his way, and was taken to court several times over debts. He considered settling in Florida but had to drop the idea, possibly as a result of his wife's lack of desire to move so far.

Having heard tales of the area known as Kentucky, Boone first travelled there in 1767. The local Native Americans had just given up their claim to the land, which was now under the British Crown. Soon after, he returned and went on a two year hunting trip, an exciting adventure that saw him captured by Indians at one point and told to leave the region. Despite this, he carried on hunting and exploring and after a brief visit home, returned for another trip.

In 1773, Boone and about fifty others set out with the intention of establishing the first permanent settlement in Kentucky. However, the Native Americans were becoming restless with so many white hunters around, and they captured and killed two of the party, including Daniel Boone's own son. As a result of this hostility the expedition was abandoned and before long full scale war had developed between Virginia and the Shawnee Indians. Boone took the job of riding around the countryside, warning others of the fact that the colony was now at war, and is estimated to have covered eight hundred miles in two months. As a result of this, and of his subsequent defence of settlements and promotion to Captain in the militia, Boone's fame began to spread.

Virginia won the war, and soon Boone was asked to find a good route that could be travelled into Kentucky. With a party of thirty or so others, he marked a trail that went through the Cumberland Gap and led to the Kentucky River, founding the town of Boonesborough. In 1775 he went back for his family and brought them to live in the new settlement.

During the American Revolution (1775-1782), local Native Americans began attacks on settlers once again, and many returned to the east. On one occasion three teenage girls, including Boone's daughter, were abducted by Indians and carried off. Boone raised a posse and ambushed the Indians, saving all three girls in what would be the most celebrated moment of his long career. However, the war with the Natives was becoming serious, and in 1777 Boone was injured in action when his kneecap was shattered by a bullet.

By 1778 Boonesborough was in a state of siege, forcing the men inside to make risky hunting trips outside of the walls, and on one of these trips they encountered a vastly superior horde of Natives. The men were forced to surrender to Chief Blackfish and his warriors. However, Boone saved his town by making a false promise to Blackfish that it would surrender as soon as spring arrived. This meant that the Indians did not make an immediate attack on the poorly defended settlement. The Shawnees adopted Boone into their family and he lived peacefully with them for a while. The following year however he learnt of an imminent attack on Boonesborough, and managed to escape and race back to the town to warn it. Over the next weeks he helped in the successful defence of the colony, even though he was viewed with suspicion by some on account of his having lived peacefully with the Shawnees.

Before long, Boone headed back east to collect his family, who had fled, and he brought more settlers back with him, forming a new town called Boone's Station. A disaster occurred when he had over $20,000 stolen from him which was supposed to be used to purchase land grants for the new pioneers. This loss would haunt him for the rest of his life. Following this, he was elected to the Virginia General Assembly and played a part in the action of the latter part of the Revolutionary War.

After the Revolution Boone tried his hand at various trades such as farming and running a hotel; his fame continued to spread, especially after a book about the settlement of Kentucky was published which included an account of Boone's expeditions. Boone County was named after him. Over time he encountered financial problems after attempting to earn money through land speculation, and he found it difficult to fit in with the new, more civilized state of the region.

By 1799 he had moved out of the United States altogether and into present day Missouri, where he spent the rest of life. He continued hunting and trapping and spent more time with his family, finally dying at the fine age of eighty-five.

Boone was a frontiersman through and through and tended to move on from an area when it became too settled for his liking. By the end of his life he was already a figure of the past, but his legend remains to this day and he is remembered especially in Kentucky as one of the first European explorers of that region.

James Harrod

A lesser known figure of the Old West, James Harrod (1746?-1792) spent time as a hunter and a soldier, but is remembered primarily for his work as a pioneer and settler in the area to the west of the Allegheny Mountains. He explored much of what is now Kentucky and Illinois, establishing Harrod's Town (present day Harrodsburg) as the first permanent settlement in Kentucky.

Harrod was born and raised in Pennsylvania, to parents John and Sarah. Little is known of his early life, though he certainly learned outdoor skills such as hunting and trapping and became a fine shot with a rifle. These were dangerous times, and indeed his brother's and father's first wives were both killed by Natives, and in 1754, during the French and Indian War (where Great Britain fought France), the family were forced to flee their home due to Indian attacks.

In 1760 he volunteered to serve under Captain Cochran, giving his age as sixteen. It has been observed that his recorded height at the time was only five feet two inches, whereas later in life he was over six foot. This suggests that he most probably lied about his age in order to be able to enlist. A few years later Harrod took part in the fighting during Pontiac's Rebellion against several Native tribes, later moving into modern day Illinois. Here he mixed with French and Indian traders and learnt to speak their languages, making contacts with other frontiersmen such as Daniel Boone.

By 1774 his reputation had grown enough for Lord Dunmore to appoint him head of an expedition to explore the area that had been promised to veterans of the French and Indian War. Harrod took thirty-seven men and travelled to the mouth of the Kentucky River, crossing Salt River into modern day Mercer County, Kentucky. Harrod's Town was established on the 16th June, and the land was divided up among the party. Harrod named his own stretch of land 'Boiling Springs'.

The settlement of the area was briefly interrupted when the men were called back for military service to fight in Lord Dunmore's War, fought against several Native tribes. However, they arrived slightly too late to take part in the hostilities, and soon Harrod returned with more settlers. Harrod's Town began to grow fast and many buildings were erected.

Harrod married Ann McDonald in 1778, after her first husband had been killed by natives. Both her father and her son from her first marriage also died at the hands of Indians, showing just how risky life on the frontier was at this time. A daughter, Margaret, was born in 1785.

During this period of his life Harrod became increasingly involved in the politics of the new region, holding the position of Justice as well as being elected to the Virginia House of Delegates. Harrod's Town became the country seat of the newly created Kentucky County, further cementing his reputation in the area. He also continued his military career, defending the region against Indian attacks and reaching the rank of Colonel.

Despite his military and political successes, and despite the fact that he was rapidly becoming a very wealthy man through the farming of his vast estate, Harrod remained a true frontiersman at heart and never fully settled down. In 1792 he left town with two other men to hunt for beaver, and never returned.

The ultimate fate of James Harrod is not known. Some speculate that he may have simply wanted to abandon his family and his old life, feeling too bogged down in the politics of the area, and that he struck out alone and lived in the wilderness. It is also possible that he was murdered by one of his companions or slain by natives. Whatever really happened, the town of Harrodsburg bears his name to this day.

DeWitt Clinton

An important though largely forgotten figure of American democracy, DeWitt Clinton (1769-1828) served in the United States Senate and was the sixth governor of New York. His lifelong interest in politics, culture and society made him influential during the latter part of the enlightenment, and helped set some of the standards of civilisation that would define the United States.

After receiving a university education, he became secretary to his uncle, George Clinton, who was serving as governor of New York. During the late eighteenth and early nineteenth century he sat on various bodies, including the New York State Assembly, the New York State Senate, the State Constitutional Convention and the Council of Appointments, the latter of which had the job of appointing all high-ranking officials in the region. In 1796 he married Maria Franklin, daughter of a wealthy local Quaker, with whom he had ten children. She died in 1818 and he soon remarried to Catherine Jones, who outlived him.

Beginning in February 1802 he sat for slightly under two years in the US Senate, but was unhappy with living conditions in Washington and so moved back to New York where he served three terms as Mayor. During this time he helped to found the Historical Society of New York and the American Academy of the Fine Arts. He was also Regent of the local university between 1808 and 1825.

Clinton was heavily involved with the Erie Canal project, which linked the Atlantic Ocean with the Great Lakes. He sat on the commission which discussed and planned the scheme, soon becoming the driving force behind it. When the canal was finished in 1825, he had the honour of officially opening it.

In 1812, Clinton ran as a candidate for President of the United States, but was defeated in a close election by James Madison. Five years later he was elected as Governor of New York, a post which he held on to in the 1820 elections. During this period it was decided that elections for Governor should be held every two years rather than three, and Clinton was not re-nominated by his party for the 1822 ballot. As a result of this he did not run and so gave up the office.

Clinton's enemies in the New York legislature voted to remove him from the Erie Canal Commission in 1824, a move that was so unpopular with the people that Clinton found himself lifted up on a wave of popular support, and as a result of this he was re-elected Governor and spent another two terms in office. He died suddenly at the age of fifty-eight, while still serving.

Clinton represents a different side of American history, a politician who gained mass support in his local region and who lived his entire life on the east coast. His successful vision of the Erie Canal, along with his social achievements, makes him a figure worth remembering.

The Alamo

The most famous event of the Texas Revolution, the Battle of the Alamo (February 23rd – March 6th 1836) is best remembered for its final day in which the Alamo Mission was overrun by Mexican forces and the defenders were massacred.

Throughout the period leading up to this event, the Mexican government had been growing more and more dictatorial and was perceived as a direct threat to the many former United States citizens who had settled in Texas, then a border region of Mexico. This led to the eventual uprising of the region and later a declaration of independence. In the early months of the war, the Texans defeated the scattered Mexican forces, causing President General Santa Anna to organise a large force to put down the rebellion. Santa Anna went further, seeking to cease the flow of United States citizens (who were flooding into Texas to aid in the revolution) by classifying all foreign combatants as pirates, meaning that they could be executed immediately upon capture.

The Alamo Mission itself was a converted religious station that had been transformed into a small fort in order to defend against Native attacks. It was certainly never intended to face up to a modern army with artillery. The Texas forces garrisoned it against the approaching Mexican army, but with fewer than one hundred men they had far too little in numbers to hold out against a determined assault. Sam Houston, one of the commanders of the Texan troops, could not spare the men to defend the fort, but sent Colonel James Bowie with thirty men in order to remove the artillery and demolish the buildings, to ensure that the enemy could not make use of them. However, this plan was soon abandoned and it was decided to stand and fight rather than withdraw. William Travis arrived with some reinforcement, as did Davy Crockett.

Travis and Bowie eventually agreed to share command of their forces, which were still woefully inadequate to mount a successful defence.

On February 23rd Mexican forces were sighted (Santa Anna had around six thousand men) and the Texan troops quickly rounded up as much food and supplies as possible and retreated into the fort. This began a siege that was to last almost two weeks. Within a few days Jim Bowie had become ill and collapsed, leaving Travis in control. There were a number of minor engagements during the siege in which the Mexicans tended to have the worst of it, but with such numerical supremacy that it hardly mattered.

By March 5th Santa Anna was preparing for a final assault, which took place the next day. The defenders repulsed two Mexican attacks, but were unable to hold off a third. In confused fighting, virtually all the Texans were killed, with a few being executed after surrendering. James Bowie, Davy Crockett and William Travis all perished in action.

Shortly after the Battle of the Alamo, the Mexican army murdered over three hundred captives at Goliad, adding to the fear and resentment with which they were viewed. However, despite being heavily outnumbered the Texan forces became even more determined to win victory. On April 21st 1863 Sam Houston led a Texan army in a complete rout of Santa Anna's troops at the Battle of San Jacinto, thus ending the war and paving the way for nationhood. Santa Anna was captured but was not executed, being eventually allowed to return home as part of a treaty.

Despite the decisive engagement of the war being fought at San Jacinto, it is the action of the Alamo that is most famous and most often described. The valiant defence of a small group of men against a large army, and the savage manner in which they died, still makes a vivid impression almost two hundred years later.

Jim Bowie

A pioneer and soldier who played an important part in the Texas revolution, James "Jim" Bowie (1796-1836) is the subject of a great amount of historical research, and an almost as large amount of mythology. Born in Logan County, Kentucky, he was the ninth of ten children born to parents who owned both horses and slaves. The family moved several times in his youth before settling in Louisiana, and the young Bowie learnt frontier skills such as hunting, trapping and planting, from a young age. He also learnt to use a pistol, rifle and various knives and developed a reputation as a skilled marksman.

In 1814 Bowie enlisted in the Louisiana militia, hoping to see military action against the British in the war that was then reaching its end; indeed, he signed up too late to be involved in the fighting and ended up working for a spell sawing lumber. After this he was involved in the Long Expedition, which attempted unsuccessfully to throw off Spanish control of Texas. He was not injured in the campaign and returned to Louisiana before Spanish reinforcements arrived in number.

Around the years 1818-1825 Bowie, after the death of his father, worked with his brother on the family estate, managing the affairs of the land, which still included slaves. In fact, they went into partnership with the pirate Jean Lafitte, smuggling slaves into the country and selling them at market in New Orleans. They made a huge amount of money in this way, and were able to move into land speculation with their profits. Teaming up with another brother, they bought and sold several estates, always managing to come out with a profit and gradually building up their capital.

Bowie's fame really began in an incident known as the Sandbar Fight. He had been involved in a feud with a local sheriff, Norris Wright, who was also a banker who had turned down a loan application from the brothers. There was an incident in which Wright fired a shot at Bowie but missed. After this Bowie swore always to carry his huge hunting knife, almost ten inches long, with him for self-defence. In September 1827, both Bowie and Wright attended a duel on a sandbank, in which they each supported a different party. The two duellists fired two shots at each other, both missed, and so the men settled their differences with a handshake. However, several fights broke out between different observers and in the confusion Wright stabbed Bowie with his sword. Despite being badly wounded, Bowie drew his knife and slashed at his opponent, killing him instantly. Following this, Bowie was stabbed and shot several more times by his other enemies in the group but somehow avoided being fatally wounded and had his wounds patched by a doctor. All the witnesses agreed that he had not struck the first blow and so there was no question of his being charged with murder. The newspapers reported on his huge weapon, and the so-called Bowie Knife rapidly gained popularity.

Having recovered from his wounds, Bowie moved to Texas, then a province of Mexico, converted to Roman Catholicism and eventually became a Mexican citizen. He became engaged to be married, but his fiancée tragically died two weeks before their wedding. In 1831 he married the daughter of one of his business partners and continued to speculate in land, with around seven hundred thousand acres passing through his hands. He also had a new scheme in mind; stories abounded of a lost Spanish silver mine somewhere in Indian territory that had been long since abandoned. Bowie received permission from the government to mount an expedition to try and recover it. Although this mission failed, it is best remembered for an incident in which the group was attacked by a Native raiding party. Bowie organised the defenders and, despite being outnumbered by something like fifteen to one, managed to drive off the Indians, losing only one man in the process. His fame continued to spread with many stories in national newspapers, although apparently

Bowie himself was a very humble man who seldom talked about his exploits.

By the early 1830s the Mexican government had begun passing laws that discriminated against American settlers in favour of those of Spanish stock. Bowie was involved with the troubles from the beginning; in 1832 he fought against the Mexican cavalry and defeated it in a small engagement, though full-scale war did not break out at this point. The Texan Revolution proper began in October 1835, and Bowie saw action at the battle of Concepcion, really more of a small-scale skirmish, in which he led a successful charge against the Mexican cannon. As the Revolution progressed and Texas declared independence, Bowie was involved in the thick of the fighting, earning much praise. However, he was denied a commission as he had made several influential enemies with his land speculation.

In 1836, Bowie was among the defenders of the Alamo, who decided to stay and resist the advancing Mexican army, despite knowing that they did not have enough men to successfully defend the fort. Although Bowie was jointly in charge of the defenders, he was struck down by a mysterious illness and was most probably confined to his bed when the fort fell. It is likely that he died fighting, albeit bedridden, and his body was later burnt along with the other defenders.

Jim Bowie is best remembered today for the enormous knife that bears his name. He seems to have been a genuinely brave man, choosing to stay and fight even when the odds were stacked against him. Though he did not have a long life, he achieved a great deal both as a soldier and as a businessman, and his fame will last.

Mountain Men

Throughout most of the nineteenth century, and especially during the early years of that period, trappers and explorers lived in the Rocky Mountains, opening up trails and making money from the fur trade. The big fur companies would hold annual fairs where hunters could sell their wares, and thus they were an important part of the American economy at the time. Mountain Men were hugely diverse, coming from all walks of life, though generally they were very independently minded having left most of civilisation behind. They tended to have good relations with local Natives and would often take an Indian wife which ensured that they remained on pleasant terms. Before the influx of settlers began to encroach on their lands the Natives had little reason to fight the white men, so peace tended to reign between them. The golden age of the Mountain Man lasted until the 1840s when western emigration and over-hunting caused the fur industry to almost collapse. After this many former explorers became army scouts and settlers, or helped guide wagon trains.

It is estimated that between 1820 and 1840 there were three thousand Mountain Men, the vast majority of whom were employed by major fur companies. The men would hunt together in well organised groups with one of them nominated as leader of the party. The companies would organise annual rendezvous at which the fur could be sold. However, the Hudson Bay Company began a policy of buying up fur cheaply, aimed at destroying the trade, and succeeded in bringing the fur companies to their knees by 1840. This coincided with a change in style in Europe, in which fur was no longer wanted. Added to these problems, the beaver was being over-hunted and becoming more and more scarce. The scale of the collapse can be seen in the number of trappers working for the Snake River Company, which was something around six hundred in 1826 but had fallen to only about fifty by 1846. The Hudson Bay Company purposely over-hunted the area to the west of the Rocky Mountains, making it unprofitable for Mountain Men to expand in that direction.

The men would hunt for animals in the summer, but waited until autumn to set their traps. They would work in groups, with each man doing a certain job, such as cooking meals or repairing damaged clothes. They tended to carry all their supplies with them and would often travel around a great deal. There were constant dangers, both human and non-human. As they were often working in unmapped areas they really had little idea what they were likely to encounter and would sometimes fight against bears or have to search for a route around suspicious Natives.

Some Mountain Men would build log cabins in the summer and use them as a home base, doing a great deal of fishing to supplement their diet. However they operated, it was a hard life, and few spent more than a handful of seasons in the wilderness. Although most were employed by major fur companies, there were a few free trappers who were effectively self-employed and who would aim to sell to the highest bidder. This was an even less stable way of life, as there was no guaranteed market, but it could prove lucrative if the conditions were right.

Although the classic age of the Mountain Man was short-lived, they are an essential part of both the myth and the reality of the Old West, and were vital in opening up overland routes and assisting the early settlers who were heading to new lands.

Lewis and Clark Expedition

In 1803 the United States purchased France's claim to the region known as Louisiana, which was effectively the middle section of the modern USA (and far larger than the present-day state Louisiana). The purchase was for the claim only and not the actual land itself, which still belonged to the local Native nations. In fact, little was known about most of the region, and so an expedition was organised to explore and map the newly 'acquired' lands. The journey had several aims, including discovering a way to reach the Pacific Ocean, finding out what natural resources were included in the area and declaring US sovereignty over local tribes.

President Thomas Jefferson named US Army Captain Meriwether Lewis as the leader of the expedition, who in turn chose William Clark as his partner. Thirty-three people set off on the mission armed with advanced weapons that were intended to impress any Indian nations that they encountered, huge amounts of supplies and special 'medals' bearing a portrait of Jefferson and a message of goodwill and peace; these were to be given out to indigenous peoples to try and calm them and establish US control in at least a nominal sense.

The group set out from their winter staging post in May 1804 and followed the Missouri river westward. During the final weeks of August they reached the edge of the Great Plains. Along the way they established relations with two dozen Indian nations, and were in fact reliant on them for help in several circumstances. The expedition would have become hopelessly lost in the Rocky Mountains were it not for local guides. There were sometimes tensions with the natives, and on one occasion the group prepared itself for battle, but things seemed to cool down at the last moment and violence was averted. In the winter of their first year, the party built Fort Mandan in present day North Dakota. Twelve months later they built Fort Clatsop in modern Oregon. On March 23rd 1806, having completed their objective of finding the Pacific Ocean, the group turned home, travelling both over land and via canoe.

On the way back, Lewis and Clark separated for a time so that each could explore a different area. Lewis' group met some men from the Blackfeet nation who tried to steal their weapons, and in the ensuing struggle two Indians were killed. Frightened of possible reprisals, they managed to travel one hundred miles in a day before making camp again. Meanwhile, Clark also had trouble as his party entered the lands of the Crow nation. During one night half of the horses were stolen, even though not a single Crow had been seen. Meeting up once more, the expedition travelled swiftly home along the Missouri River, reaching St Louis on September 23rd 1806.

The Lewis and Clark expedition was important in giving the US its first accurate view of the North-West, including about one hundred and forty maps. The group documented natural resources, including some plants and even animals that had been unknown to the white man; around two hundred new species were discovered. In addition, over seventy Indian tribes were noted, allowing for much greater diplomatic and expansionist policies in the following years. All in all, the expedition was the first step in the opening up of the West.

Sacagawea

A Lemhi Shoshone woman, Sacagawea (1788-1812) accompanied the Lewis and Clark Expedition, acting as an interpreter and guide. With the party, she travelled thousands of miles from North Dakota to the Pacific Ocean between 1804 and 1806. She was nicknamed Janey by Clark. Although reliable information about her is very limited, she captured the public imagination, especially in the early years of the twentieth century when the American Women's Suffrage Association adopted her as a symbol of female worth and independence, erecting several statues in her memory.

Sacagawea was pregnant with her first child when the expedition arrived near her village in the winter of 1804. She was the wife of Toussaint Charbonneau, a Quebecer trapper who was living in the village. Lewis and Clark had interviewed several trappers who could act as potential guides, but hired Charbonneau when they found that his wife could speak Shoshone, as they knew that they would need the help of Shoshone tribes at the headwater of the Missouri. Soon after, the married couple moved into the expedition's fort, and Sacagawea gave birth to a healthy son who would accompany her on the epic trip.

In April the party left the fort and headed up the Missouri River. On May 14th 1805 Sacagawea rescued several items that had fallen from an upturned boat, including vital journals. As a reward for her quick action, the section of river was named after her. Shortly after this she negotiated with local Shoshone, managing to make an agreement where the Indians would barter horses and also lead the party over the Rocky Mountains, a route which would have been virtually impossible unaided.

On the return trip through the Rockies, Sacagawea discovered that she knew the area quite well, and led the party to a gap in the mountains, now known as Gibbons Pass. Shortly afterwards she successfully advised the expedition to cross into the Yellowstone River basin at what is now Bozeman Pass; this was much later chosen as the route which the Northern Pacific Railway would take. Although she only offered advice on a few occasions, Sacagawea was vital in negotiating peaceful settlement with the indigenous people who were encountered. It is likely that the very presence of a native woman served a useful purpose in advertising their non-violent intent.

Following the expedition, Charbonneau and Sacagawea lived for a while among the Hidatsa people, before accepting an invitation from Clark to settle in St Louis, Missouri in 1809. Sacagawea probably died in 1812, having given birth to a daughter two years previously. The Lewis and Clark expedition played a key role in opening up the West, and the young Shoshone woman was an important part of it.

Jim Bridger

A mountain man, trapper and scout, Jim Bridger (1804-1881) was one of the most important explorers of the western United States. He began his career when young, signing on for General William Ashley's Upper Missouri Expedition at the age of eighteen. As one of the first white men to reach what is now Yellowstone, he saw the natural wonders of the region, including the geysers. In 1825 he became the first non Native American to see the Great Salt Lake in modern day Utah, initially believing it to be a part of the Pacific Ocean.

By 1830 Bridger was moving into business and established the Rocky Mountain Fur Company, along with a few associates. They concentrated on selling beaver pelts for which there was a considerable market. In 1843 he built a trading post which later grew and became known as Fort Bridger. Married three times to Native women and widowed twice, Bridger fathered several children whom he sent back to the east so that they could receive a good education.

Making more explorations, Bridger left his name on the landscape. In 1850 he scouted a mountain pass which he called Bridger's Pass, shortening the Oregon Trail by over sixty miles. The route was so successful that the railroad was later built through it. In 1864 he forged the Bridger Trail, leading from Wyoming to the Montana goldfields, which made for a far safer journey through less dangerous terrain than the established routes.

Later, Bridger used his knowledge of the local area to aid the army as a scout during the first Powder River expedition, against hostile Natives who had been attacking travellers. When his role in the conflict ended, in 1865, he returned to Missouri and settled down to a less adventurous life. Plagued by health problems in his final decades, he died in 1881.

As a living legend of the Old West, Bridger was well known for telling stories, some true and some fictional. He loved to have an audience and, especially in his later years, would talk for hours about his exploits, often leaving his listeners wondering whether what they had just heard was true or not. For example, when he told about the geysers of Yellowstone, many people thought that it was nothing more than a tall tale, for the idea of water shooting out of the ground seemed just too much to believe.

A good number of places in the modern United States bear Bridger's name, and he remains the quintessential frontiersman well over a century after his death.

Cochise

A Native American Apache chief, Cochise (1805?-1874) is often ranked alongside Geronimo as one of the most important and well-known Apache leaders of the Old West. His name translates to something like 'Man with the Strength of Oak'. His people ranged over the land that is now northern Mexico and southern United States, and had for centuries been defending their region against the white man, usually with a good measure of success. By the time Cochise was born the Mexicans had started targeting Apache civilians and offering a bounty on scalps; Cochise's own father was killed by bounty hunters, which greatly increased his son's resolve to fight the invaders.

Having spent the first decades of his life fighting Mexicans, Cochise and the local Apache experienced a brief period of peace in the 1850s when the land was acquired by the United States. Cochise does not seem to have fought battles for the sake of battles, and was happy enough to live in peace when the opportunity presented itself. However, as white settlers encroached on Native land, tensions began to run high and it was only a matter of time before trouble erupted.

In 1861 an Apache raiding party captured a local rancher's son. Cochise was accused of this incident despite being completely innocent; in fact another branch of the Apache was responsible. Being invited to the army headquarters to discuss what had occurred, Cochise offered to look into the matter and try to bring those responsible to justice. However, the army had other ideas and decided that the chief should be arrested. Realising what was about to happen, Cochise drew a knife and fought his way out of the meeting tent, escaping without several members of his family who were taken as prisoners. Following this incident there were unsuccessful negotiations as the Apaches and whites attempted to trade hostages. Tragically, all the prisoners on both sides were eventually killed as no settlement was reached. As a result of this the whole region exploded in violence with raids and counter raids frequently taking place. In general the Apache had the upper hand in these conflicts, striking quickly and then escaping before reinforcements could arrive.

The only pitched battle that Cochise fought against the US army was at Apache Pass in 1862; he and about five hundred warriors fought the whites to a standstill, until artillery fire was brought to bear. This was the first time that the Apache had faced artillery, and despite holding out for a surprising amount of time they were eventually forced to flee. The following year US forces captured Cochise's father-in-law, under the pretence of a truce, and later murdered him. This, along with other incidents of broken promises, convinced the Apache leadership that the whites could not be trusted, as they seemed to break every promise that they made.

As time progressed Cochise and his men were forced back to the Dragoon Mountains, where they were able to hold out and continue raiding. However, in 1872 a treaty was masterminded by Tom Jeffords, a white man who became good friends with the Apache, and both sides stuck to the treaty for the remaining years of Cochise's life. The old chief died of cancer a couple of years later.

For all the savagery of war, Cochise showed that he was willing to sign and abide by treaties, even when it seemed that the white men would never stick by the agreements. The brief periods of peace that occurred in his time show that he was no war-mad leader, but was genuinely attempting to allow his people to continue their traditional way of life; if his was an often violent existence then we must remember that these were hugely violent times.

Movies

The history of western movies, also known as Horse Operas, runs parallel to the history of the cinema itself. Cinematic cameras were invented just as the period of the Old West was drawing to a close, and before long short cowboy films were enjoying mass popularity. Writers such as Ned Buntline had long before invented the western genre with their dime novels, and early films were a simple case of building upon this foundation. The classic age of the Western was the 1930s to the 1960s, but they have continued to enjoy popularity up to the present day. The first ever proper film in this genre is generally considered to be The Great Train Robbery, from 1903, which lasted for around ten minutes.

Westerns focus on the frontier between civilisation and the wilderness, and are most often set in the time between the Civil War and the dawning of the Twentieth Century. They are sometimes set earlier, however, and quite often take place around the events of the Texas War of Independence and the Battle of the Alamo in the 1830s. A regular focus is on the taming of nature, the settlement of new land and the troubles that occur between different groups of pioneers. Settings often include isolated forts or homesteads, wagon trains, the saloon, the jail, the stables, the main street of a small town and sometimes Native American camps or villages. Westerns also frequently involve a number of iconic elements such as a hanging judge and hanging tree, colourful cowboys with spurs and lassoes, gunfights, bandannas and buckskins, stagecoaches, gambling, card play, cattle drives, prostitutes, land grabbing and more.

Often the theme of the movie deals with law enforcement, telling a fast-paced story of 'good guys' versus 'bad'. The characters are frequently very clear-cut between heroes and villains, though some films, especially more modern ones, do involve complex characters who can grow and change. Quite often the hero faces a large number of bad guys and is forced to deal with them alone, showing off his skills with a gun.

The western usually mixes myth and reality in order to create an exciting narrative with plenty of action. One good example of this is in the fact that heroes and heroines are often able to shoot with ridiculous accuracy, and often while running or riding a horse. In actual fact, although it was true that most people carried guns, it was only a tiny specialist proportion of the population who really knew how to use them. Most people who were killed in gun fights were shot at very close range, often from behind as they were taken by surprise.

A feature that has changed a great deal across the years is the treatment of Native Americans. In early films they tended to be shown in a very negative light, often as little more than savages whose only real role was to be killed by whites. As time has progressed, movie makers have begun to explore the Indians in more detail, producing films that take a more rounded approach and deal with them as human beings and as characters in their own right.

The enduring popularity of the Western shows that it is a genre which is likely to continue and be explored in new ways in future years. The rich mixture of truth and fantasy, set amid rugged terrain, seems to appeal to audiences in a timeless manner.

Winchester Rifle

Among the earliest repeating rifles, Winchester models were instrumental in the hands of western settlers, with especially the '73 design being known as 'the gun that won the west'. Lever action weapons, they were manufactured by the Winchester Repeating Arms Company, founded by Oliver Fisher Winchester (1810-1880), a world-renowned New England industrialist. As well as the rifle-making company he also founded the Yale National Bank and the New Haven Water Company. He was elected lieutenant governor of Connecticut in 1866.

The first such gun was the 1866 model, famed for its rugged construction which made it extremely hard to damage, as well as its lever action mechanism which meant that a number of shots could be fired before having to reload. This is where the term 'repeating rifle' comes from. The new patent improved flaws in the earlier Henry rifle by using a loading gate on the side of the frame and a round sealed magazine, covered by a fore stock. This version was nicknamed Yellow Boy because of the brass effect receiver, which was actually a bronze alloy called gunmetal.

The most famous incarnation, the 1873 design, was produced so that it could be fired with popular handgun cartridges of the day. Eventually a 'Frontier Model' was designed that used the same ammunition as the single action army Peacemaker, allowing cowboys and other frontier types to carry just one kind of bullet for both their rifle and pistol. The weapon was produced and used in huge quantities, thus gaining the nickname of 'the gun that won the west' and inspiring many dime novelists to base stories around its performance. Many decades later, in 1950, a film was produced called Winchester '73, starring James Stewart, which shows how the legacy of the gun continued well into the twentieth century.

The 1876 model was a heavier-framed version than the previous incarnations, and was chambered for full-powered centre fire rifle cartridges, rather than rim fire cartridges or handgun sized rounds. It was actually based on an earlier prototype design, from 1868, that had never been commercially released. The gun was introduced to celebrate the nation's hundredth birthday, and was generally considered to be a well built and accurate hunting rifle. It was the only repeater to have been used in large numbers by professional buffalo hunters, and was also issued to the Texas Rangers. Future president Theodore Roosevelt used a '76 on his early hunting expeditions to the west.

The 1886 version continued moving towards chambering heavier rounds and incorporated a stronger locking-block action, meaning that it could hold very heavy ammunition. It was designed by John Moses Browning who worked with Winchester for many years. The next model was the 1892, which returned to the use of shorter, lower pressure handgun rounds, making something of a reunion with the earlier designs. Two years later, John Browning completed the '94 version which was chambered for new, smokeless propellants, the first civilian firearm to use this technology. This edition went on to become one of the bestselling guns of all time and was immensely popular with hunters. The final model of the nineteenth century was the 1895, which loaded from a box magazine instead of from a tube under the barrel. It was chambered for military cartridges with pointed projectiles and was used by the armies of a number of nations including Great Britain and Russia.

Although it is the '73 version which is most well remembered, Winchester had a long track record of producing guns that could achieve both a high rate of fire and a fine accuracy. The weapons were particularly effective against Native Americans, who were often taken by surprise upon finding that virtually no reloading time was needed, allowing rifle-armed men in defensive positions to wreak havoc on attacking forces. The sheer defensive ability also foreshadowed the Great War of the early twentieth century, where dug-in forces would be almost unbreakable. For the nineteenth century though, they truly were the guns that won the west.

Colt Peacemaker

A single action revolver, with a cylinder holding six metallic cartridges, the Colt Single Action Army, also known as the Peacemaker, was originally designed for the US government service revolver trials of 1873 by Colt's Patent Firearms Manufacturing Company. The weapon was popular in the Old West with everyone from ranchers to lawmen to outlaws, making it a truly iconic gun of the time. Along with the Winchester repeating rifles, it was vital in exploring and conquering the west.

The weapon was manufactured in several barrel lengths, including a short 'Civilian' model, a longer 'Artillery' design and an even longer 'Cavalry' version. There was also a model with a very short barrel and no ejector rod, often known as a 'Sheriff's model' or 'Banker's special'.

The peacemaker is a refined version of various earlier models, including the Colt Percussion and the Colt 1871. Mounted on a central axis, the cylinder is operated by a 'hand' with a double 'finger' whose extended action allows the cylinder ratchet to be cut in a large circle, giving more force to the cylinder. To fire the gun the hammer must be drawn to full cock and the trigger pulled. It is theoretically possible to fire the weapon rapidly, when the trigger is held down and the hammer quickly 'fanned'. Although this is common practice in movies, in real life it is very inaccurate, rather dangerous and likely to damage the mechanism of the gun, leaving expensive repairs needed.

The term 'single action' refers to the behaviour of the trigger. Its hammer must be cocked manually before each shot, and the trigger only performs a single action in releasing the hammer. Most modern revolvers are 'double action' as pulling the trigger will both cock and release the hammer. As with most contemporary revolvers, the Colt could hold six rounds, but one was normally left empty for safety purposes. This is because a forceful blow to the hammer could discharge one of the rounds by accident, which was clearly far too dangerous to allow.

Quite a few famous names of the Old West used a Peacemaker, most notably Wyatt Earp; the fine mixture of ease of use, accuracy and stopping power was a winning combination for many. Today the original guns are rare and extremely expensive collector's editions, but at the time they were devastatingly powerful weapons, capable of dispatching enemies with frightening power.

John Charles Fremont

Famous both as an explorer and as the first presidential candidate of the anti-slavery Republican Party, John Charles Fremont (1813-1890) was known in his day as 'The Great Pathfinder'. His career in both exploration and politics was often controversial, and he remains an intriguing figure to the modern era.

Following his education at the College of Charleston between 1829 and 1831, Fremont spent some time as a teacher of mathematics aboard a naval sloop. In 1838 he was appointed a second lieutenant in the Corps of Topographical Engineers, assigned to lead multiple surveying expeditions through the western United States. One of his first major assignments was to explore the lands between the Mississippi and Missouri rivers. He later mapped the Des Moines River as well. An important event in his life occurred in 1842, when he met frontiersman Kit Carson on a Missouri steam boat in St Louis. At the time, Fremont was looking for a guide to South Pass in the Rocky Mountains and Carson volunteered for the role. The five month journey was a success, and all twenty-five men returned safely. Between 1842 and 1846 the two men worked together in exploring the Oregon Trail and Sierra Nevada; Fremont became the first American to see Lake Tahoe and also mapped volcanoes such as Mount St Helens.

In the mid '40s Congress published Fremont's 'Report and Map' which guided thousands of overland immigrants to Oregon and California. Shortly afterwards a man named Joseph Ware printed his "Emigrants' Guide to California", largely drawn from Fremont's work, that was a guide to the masses of hopeful prospectors during the Gold Rush.

In June 1845, Fremont and Carson left St Louis with fifty-five men, aiming to locate the source of the Arkansas River on the east side of the Rocky Mountains. However, as soon as they reached Arkansas Fremont had a change of heart and led his expedition to Mexican controlled California instead. Arriving in the Sacramento Valley he sought to stir up patriotic enthusiasm among American settlers, hoping that they would declare themselves independent. This naturally caused trouble with Mexican troops, which soon forced the expedition to flee. There was also trouble with Natives and the party became involved in bitter fighting with some Klamath people; at one point Fremont saved Carson's life by riding down an Indian who was about to shoot him with a poison arrow.

Starting in 1846, Fremont led men in the Mexican-American War and was generally successful, eventually being appointed as military governor of California. However, he was later replaced but refused to give up his position; this eventually led to him being court-martialled and convicted of mutiny and disobeying a superior officer. Despite this, the President commuted his sentence of dishonourable discharge, and he resigned his military positions.

In 1848 Fremont led another expedition, this time to find a route for a proposed railroad that would link St Louis and San Francisco along the 38th parallel. He took thirty-five men with him, and they embarked up the Missouri, Kansas and Arkansas rivers. On reaching Bent's Fort, he was advised by most of the trappers not to continue the journey as winter was coming in and there was already a foot of snow on the ground. Despite these warning he insisted that they continue, although several of the expedition quit and turned for home. Attempting to scale mountains in the icy cold and under many feet of snow, the party were soon exhausted and in deep trouble; by the time they crawled into Taos, New Mexico, ten men were dead, along with a large number of the animals.

Moving into politics, Fremont served for a few months as one of the first senators of California, and in 1856 he stood as the first presidential candidate of the new Republican Party, running on a strong anti-slavery ticket. He ended up coming second to James Buchanan in a three way race, failing to win the state of California. When the Civil War began, he served as a major-general in the Union forces, imposing martial law in Missouri and emancipating slaves there. This proved to be too much for President Abraham Lincoln, who relieved him of his command. Fremont continued to serve during much of the war, eventually moving to New York.

Fremont ran for president again in 1864, this time standing against the Republican Lincoln for the Radical Republicans, a group of hard-line abolitionists who feared that the President was not going far enough on the issue. However, he eventually abandoned his campaign after striking a deal with his opponents. In later life, Fremont dabbled in business, including railroad ownership, and spent time as governor of the Arizona territory. He eventually moved back to New York and, by the time of his death, was largely forgotten. Despite this he regained his fame in the twentieth century and is now seen as a very important, if often controversial, explorer and statesman.

California Gold Rush

One of the great phenomena of nineteenth-century America, the California Gold Rush (1848-1855) began when a man named James W. Marshall discovered gold at Sutter's Mill in Coloma, California. As news of the find spread like wildfire, over three hundred thousand people eventually made their way to the region, around half of whom came by land and half by sea. The gold hunters were known as forty-niners, the name coming from the year 1849 in which the rush really began to gather momentum.

Considerable hardships were faced by many on the trip, as those travelling by land had to put up with rough conditions, harsh weather and the ever present danger of attack by Natives or outlaws. As a means of protecting themselves, many made the journey in groups, and wagon trains heading west became a common sight. Travelling by boat was not much better, as people crowded into small berths and suffered from terrible sea sickness. As well as those from the USA, tens of thousands came from Latin America and Europe, and even as far away as Australia and China, as the rush became a truly international event.

To begin with, simple techniques were used to find the gold, such as panning, but before long this developed into full scale mining. By 1853 hydraulic mining was being used, in which a high pressure hose directed a powerful jet of water at gold-bearing gravel beds. The loosened gravel and gold would then pass over sluices, with the gold settling to the bottom where it was collected. The development of more advanced methods of gold seeking led to an increase in the cost required to begin in the first place, and this led to individuals being gradually replaced by large companies that could finance the initial outlay.

California itself was originally part of Mexico, but after the Mexican-American War of the 1840s it had won its independence and joined the USA. The huge amount of immigration during the gold rush meant that there were soon demands for it to be made a full state, and this was granted in 1850. The rush affected the area in many other ways; hundreds of roads, churches and schools were built, along with many new towns. San Francisco grew from a small settlement into a major boom town, beginning its growth into the metropolis that it is today. On a darker note, it is estimated that around one hundred thousand Indians died as a result of the events, as they were gradually pushed off their land by the new settlers. New diseases such as smallpox, measles and influenza claimed many native lives, and as mining debris choked up the rivers, fish died and game disappeared. In 1850 an act was passed allowing for the virtual enslavement of Indians and many were forced into indentured service.

New transportation methods developed as steam ships came into regular service and railroads were built. Agriculture and ranching expanded throughout the state and within a few years the whole region was irreversibly altered. The end result of all this expansion was that California became the light of the west, a beacon that encouraged others to move into new frontiers and settle fresh lands. The gold rush was vitally important in opening up the west and setting the eyes of the people towards the new territories. As for those who had hunted for gold, some hit the jackpot and made a fortune, while others ended up with little more than what they had started with. Greed, one of the great motivators of human beings, had played its part in history.

Ned Buntline

Edward Judson (1813-1886), is known to the world as Ned Buntline, the name which he used for his writing. He is best remembered today for his numerous dime novels which explored and mythologized the Old West, creating a popular genre of fiction that continues to be influential to this day.

Born in New York, Judson ran away from home at a young age and signed on with the navy as a cabin boy. At the age of thirteen he was instrumental in the rescue of the crew of a sinking ship which had been hit by a ferry, and as a result of this he received a commission as a midshipman. His fellow midshipmen were not keen on this new recruit, given his age and background, and Judson ended up fighting several duels against them, always coming out on top. He saw a small amount of action in the Seminole Wars, in which several Native tribes were in conflict with the United States army. After some years he resigned from the navy, though much later, during the Civil War, he would serve in a mounted rifle unit.

Taking the name Buntline (a nautical term), he published his first story in 1838. Working on the east coast he attempted to move into full time literary work and started up several newspapers and short story regulars, but met with little success. Most of his business ventures folded, though a weekly story paper titled 'Ned Buntline's Own' was formed in 1848 and met with enough enthusiasm to keep going, giving him a regular place for his writings and opinions.

In 1849 Buntline was involved in the Astor Place Riot, a dark day in American history in which feelings of resentment against foreigners boiled over and in the ensuing chaos twenty-three people were killed. Buntline had been involved in stirring up ethnic hatred and as a result was fined $250 and sentenced to a year in jail. He served his time and, upon release, continued to write fiction for numerous magazines and periodicals. He also continued publishing the dime novels that would make him famous. His work gradually came to be respected and enjoyed, and he was able to make quite a lot of money for his efforts. Also, he became involved in the temperance movement and gave lectures on the evil of alcohol. Despite this, he is known to have been a heavy drinker himself!

Later in life, Buntline became fascinated by Wild Bill Hickok and desperately wanted to write a book about him. He finally caught up with Hickok in Nebraska, but was threatened with a gun and told to leave town within twenty-four hours. Clearly Wild Bill did not want the attention, but Buntline was not put off and began to look for other ways to research his hero. It was during one such research expedition that he met Buffalo Bill and his Wild West Show, and was so impressed with him that he gave up the idea of writing about Hickok and decided to write about Buffalo Bill instead.

Buntline's series of novels about his new friend were hugely successful, and he and Buffalo Bill eventually performed together in a play called 'Scouts of the Prairie' in Chicago. The play was a big success with audiences despite being panned by critics; however, Buffalo Bill found Buntline hard work and did not see a future for them in performance, so before long they went their separate ways.

After his adventures with Bill, Buntline returned to writing and continued with his series of dime novels. His later books had a reasonable audience despite not being as well received as his earlier works, and he was a fairly wealthy man when he finally died from a heart attack in 1886.

Ned Buntline was not a great author in the classic sense, but his stories and novels do evoke both the reality and the myth of the great American West. He therefore played a large part in how future generations would come to view his age.

Samuel Colt

An inventor and industrialist of the first order, Samuel Colt (1814-1862) was the founder of Colt's Patent Fire-Arms Manufacturing Company, and is widely credited with popularising the revolver. His work is universally held to have greatly shaped the production and use of American firearms.

Born in Hartford, Connecticut, Colt grew up working in farming and attended a local school. From a young age he would prefer to read scientific encyclopaedias rather than concentrating on Bible study; in particular he had a book called 'Compendium of Knowledge' which, importantly, contained articles on gunpowder. He also read about the inventor Robert Fulton who inspired him to always aim for high standards in his work. Later, he overheard soldiers talking about the success of the double barrelled rifle; these same men then went on to discuss how it would be impossible to ever produce a gun capable of firing five or six rounds. At this point, Colt decided that he would aim for the 'impossible' and create just such a gun. Working in his father's textile plant he had access to tools and carried out some early experiments. He also spent some time at sea, and later claimed that his observation of the ship's wheel inspired his first design for a revolver. During the voyage, he made a wooden version of his earliest gun. Returning home, Colt went to work with his father and produced two prototype revolvers; however they were not successful as the older Colt thought that the idea was essentially foolish and so used only very cheap materials which did not perform well.

After spending some time travelling around Europe and showcasing his ideas, Colt returned to the United States and took out a patent on a 'revolving gun', being granted this in February 1836. For all his technical genius, Colt did not claim to have invented the revolver, as his gun was essentially a more practical version of Collier's revolving flintlock, which had achieved great popularity in England. However, he invented the assembly line method of production in order to reduce the cost of the finished product, understanding that his invention would never be popular if the price was too high. He also conceived of the idea of interchangeable parts, meaning that if one section of the gun needed replacing it would not mean that an entirely new weapon had to be purchased.

Despite a successful meeting with President Andrew Jackson, which resulted in a Congress bill being passed allowing for military testing of the gun, Colt met with a major setback when the production time of his new revolver was too slow, causing orders to be cancelled; furthermore, it was illegal for state legislatures to allocate funding to weapons not being currently used by federal troops. Although Colt did manage to supply troops in Florida with some of the guns, the unusual design led to problems, and a massive economic crash eventually forced his factory to close.

After spending some time developing underwater telegraph wires and navel mines, Colt returned to gun manufacturing when Captain Samuel Walker ordered one-thousand revolvers to use in the Mexican-American War. This large order allowed production to begin once again. No longer having a factory, Colt hired Eli Whitney Blake, a man well established in the firearms business, to make his guns. The new weapons were a success and soon an order came in for a thousand more. Finally meeting with triumph, Colt founded his own manufacturing company and was able to cash in on the California gold rush and the general western expansion, in which his guns became widely popular at last. Having a monopoly over the production and sale of the revolver, he was able to expand his factory several times and also to break into the European market in which he found further success.

Purchasing a large tract of land beside the Connecticut River, Colt built a new factory, a manor for himself and a large amount of housing for his employees. He introduced a ten hour working day with a one hour lunch break, quite enlightened for the time, and founded a club for employees to relax in. He married in 1856, and lived the remaining years of his life as a hugely influential manufacturer and inventor. By the time of his death he had around $15,000,000; a staggering sum for the day.

Samuel Colt has a central part in the story of the Old West and later American history. His revolvers revolutionised the art of gunnery and made it possible for US troops to suddenly gain a large advantage over Indian nations. His desire to make an 'impossible' gun and his dogged determination in carrying out the project make him a figure to be admired in a violent age.

Samuel Walker

Samuel Walker (1817-1847) was a Texas Ranger and officer of the armies of the Texas Republic and the United States. Born in Maryland, he came to Texas in 1842 to defend against a Mexican invasion. He joined the Rangers in 1844 and was soon promoted to Captain.

Acting on his own initiative, Walker went to New York to meet famous gun manufacturer Samuel Colt. He proposed a new weapon based on the then popular five-shot Colt Paterson revolver, but with a number of enhancements, such as a sixth chamber. The new gun soon went into production and the United States Mounted Rifle Companies were equipped with them in 1847.

In its day, the Walker-Colt was the largest and most powerful handgun ever created. The weapon was a six shooter and was designed to be particularly effective at close range. Only 1,100 of the guns were originally produced, making them incredibly valuable today. The original order called for only one thousand, but the manufacturer Eli Whitney Junior, produced an additional one hundred for private sales and gifts.

The powder charge of the Walker-Colt was over twice that of a normal black-powder revolver, and this could cause problems with ruptured cylinders as the weapon went off with such a big explosion. It also suffered from an inadequate loading lever catch that often allowed the lever to drop during recoil, preventing fast follow-up shots. Before long further contracts were made to create more guns, and the design was improved in various ways, such as reducing the charge from sixty to fifty grams to make the weapon more manageable, and the addition of a positive catch at the end of the loading lever to prevent the dropping of the lever under recoil.

Sadly, Walker did not live long enough to see his gun in much action. In 1847 he was killed with a lance while fighting a duel against the Mayor of the city of Huamantla during the Mexican-American War. It is said that he died with two of his beloved guns in his hands, though whether this is true or just a myth is uncertain.

Horses

The most basic form of travel aside from walking, journeying by horseback was very common in the Old West, and many people would have either owned their own horse or borrowed one from time to time as the need arose. Sometimes a livery stable would offer horses and wagons for hire, but would also allow owners to 'board' their horses there for a fee. Sometimes full livery was offered, in which the horses were fed and watered and also taken out for exercise. Part livery, on the other hand, involved the horses being fed and mucked out, but nothing further. The very cheapest option was usually known as a 'do it yourself' routine, in which the rider was simply presented with a stable and left to look after all the needs of the horse himself.

Although not native to North America since prehistoric times, the horse spread rapidly after being introduced by European settlers in the fifteenth and sixteenth century. As the occasional animal escaped and bred in the wilderness, they began to fan out across the continent and some Native tribes discovered them long before they had any contact with whites. In fact, by the time settlers encountered them, some Indians had tamed horses generations before and were already using them as a central part of their way of life. None the less, it must have been a shock when they saw their first horse; it is said that the people of the Aztec Empire thought that rider and steed were one centaur-like creature when they first saw mounted Europeans.

The horse was used not only for travel but for all manner of other activities, including playing a vital role in the lives of cowboys and others involved in cattle drives. Some owners would treat their mounts as little more than tools, whereas others would take very good care of them, valuing them for their company as well as their other uses. Many famous figures of the Old West had good relations with their horses, seeing them as an essential part of their lifestyle and existence. The horse also frequently plays a key role in western films and novels. Often the hero or villain has a favourite mount, and sometimes fights and duels break out over the ownership of a particular animal.

Free roaming, wild horses of North America are known as Mustangs; around 1900 it was estimated that there were over two million of them on the continent, though numbers have dropped greatly since then. The Mustang plays an important part in the history and legacy of the Old West, as large herds of wild horses that could be caught and tamed were very much a feature of the plains.

The golden age of horse travel survived the railways and other modern transport inventions in the nineteenth-century, still being used by millions of Americans right up to the 1900s. It was only gradually, with the coming of the motor car, that horseback travel began to slowly fade away. These days many do still use horses, but their time as the primary means of transport is little but a distant memory.

Spurs

Spurs are metal tools designed to be worn in pairs on the heels of riding boots, used to direct a horse to move forward while riding it. They are intended to back up other methods of controlling the animal, such as vocal commands, use of the legs and hands, and suchlike. Spurs are usually held on by a leather strap that goes over the arch of the foot and under the sole in front of the boot heel.

In the Old West many people would own at least one horse, and it was often the easiest means of transport, especially in rural areas and before the railroad started to become popular. This meant that spurs were quite important, and were often seen as more than just a tool and as an actual piece of personal kit that one could use to show off with. The most common design was known as a rowelled spur and had a toothed wheel which spun, with the teeth being quite blunt so as not to hurt the animal. These would sometimes be decorated with designs or made with bright colours and tended to be highly prized among 'horse' types, such as cowboys and pioneers.

Most characters in the Old West took great care of their horses and would not have wanted to hurt them, so spurs were sometimes known as 'gentle persuaders' as they were designed simply to prompt the animal and not to cause it any actual pain. In fact, it has been said of several outlaws that they had more respect for horses than they did for men, and this is probably not too much of an exaggeration.

Today, the spur is still considered an essential part of western dress; it also plays a small but significant part in many movies, in which it is important to show characters wearing the correct gear. All in all, the spur was more than a device to be used to control a horse and was a symbol of the friendly relation between man and animal that was so vital to old America.

Steam Boats

A steam boat is a ship in which propulsion is mainly achieved through steam power, usually driving propellers or a paddle wheel. During the Old West they were primarily seen working on lakes and rivers, gaining great popularity during the nineteenth century and very quickly replacing sailing ships for commercial haulage. Despite this, steam boats usually still had auxiliary sails in case of emergencies, though these were very rarely used.

The first recorded steam boat in North America was built in 1787 by a man named John Fitch. A few years later Samuel Morey demonstrated his own creation on the Connecticut River, becoming the first to successfully use a paddle wheel. However, the steam boat was first used commercially by Robert Fulton, who as a young man had visited Europe and been inspired by the advances in technology that he saw there. Back in America, in 1807, he began to operate a route linking New York City and Albany, which could traverse the one hundred and fifty miles in thirty-six hours. Soon, other commercially minded people were setting up their own companies and their own routes, spreading rapidly across the continent into rivers and the Great Lakes. In 1811 a route opened from Pittsburgh to New Orleans, travelling via the Ohio and Mississippi rivers, and is still in operation today. A boat known as Ontario was specially made to run on Lake Ontario and the surrounding region.

The use of steam boats exploded in the years leading up to the Civil War, both in terms of commercial and passenger use. They were also quite a dangerous way to travel at times. Apart from the sometimes unsavoury customers who would be in transit from one place to another, there was always the risk of a boiler explosion or some other kind of potentially fatal mishap occurring. A journey on board one of these new boats could be anything from relaxing to chaotic, depending on which boat you were on, who else was on board, and what kind of services it was offering. There would often be a good deal of drinking and gambling going on as passengers looked to idle away time, and fights would naturally break out every now and again, with murders not unknown.

The steam boats had a large and positive effect on the American economy in the nineteenth century, replacing wagons and river vehicles as the primary means of commercial transport. Before the age of steam, most goods were transported down rivers via rafts, flatboats and keelboats, but these methods were slow and expensive. With the new technology shipping costs were greatly reduced, the whole process was speeded up and became considerably less dangerous. Two developers of the steam boat, Robert Fulton and Robert Livingston, attempted to secure monopoly rights over the usage of the steam boats in the western rivers; however, their attempt was blocked by the courts. This meant that an open and competitive market remained. As goods could be shipped at cheaper rates, the savings were passed on to customers, making everybody happy. Furthermore, new jobs were created as engineers and navigators were required to make each run go smoothly. It was generally held that the sooner a town developed its own steam boat service, the sooner it would prosper.

The steam boat eventually declined, due to the advance of diesel powered vessels in the twentieth century. Despite this they remain iconic of travel in old America.

Stagecoaches

A stagecoach is a covered wagon used for transporting goods and passengers, usually drawn by four horses. Used widely in America before the introduction of railroads, they made regular trips between stations, which were places of rest for passengers. Those undertaking a long journey would travel between several stations as they progressed. The first wagons were used in the eighteenth-century, generally crude affairs that needed a great deal of maintenance to keep them road worthy; the first routes were opened in New England in 1744, and these were followed by a New York to Philadelphia link in 1756. Towards the end of the century, mail coaches appeared to replace the older mail riders, carrying both post and passengers. By 1829, Boston had over seventy coach routes passing through it.

Certain routes were shut down after steam boats began operations, but the coaches still had an important part to play in relaying passengers from their homes to the docks. Likewise, when railroads began to become the principal means of long distance travel, coaches were still required to take people to and from the nearest station, so to a certain extent they managed to find a niche role even in a rapidly modernising society.

The first Concord stagecoach was built in 1827, and made a number of improvements on the general design, particularly using leather strap braces underneath the vehicle which gave it a swinging motion instead of jumping up and down on a spring suspension. Concord coaches were so solid and reliably built that it was said that they never broke down but simply wore out.

Most vehicles were nowhere near as comfortable as Concord designs. In coaches with three bench seats the passengers had to ride three abreast and were squeezed into a space of about fifteen inches each. The back and middle rows both faced forward, while the forward row faced rearwards. Those in the forward and middle row had to ride with their knees dovetailed. Passengers on the centre seat had only a leather strap to support their backs, which was very uncomfortable on a long journey. Baggage usually had to be carried personally, on one's lap, and sometimes mail pouches were stuffed beneath passengers' feet. There was always the threat of becoming ill from motion sickness and the constant jarring of the bumpy road.

Some journeys would last as long as three weeks, with time spent in baking heat and freezing cold, with poor food and hardly any rest, crowded into a tiny space. There was also a serious risk of attack from both highwaymen and Native Americans. As coaches often carried vast amounts of money being transferred from one place to another, they naturally made a fine target for robbers, meaning that a large number would either be held up or forced to defend themselves. In fact it was often recommended that each passenger bring a rifle, a pistol and plenty of ammunition with them. The danger of Indian attack depended largely on the current state of relations between whites and natives, but at times it could be very hazardous; when Cochise began his war to drive settlers out of Apache lands, six coaches were captured and burnt and all the passengers killed.

As well as delivery services, the coaches provided an important link between cities and other areas of civilisation at a time when communications were usually very poor. Especially before the dominance of trains, news would travel via stage and would thus have the effect of linking up different parts of the country. Even after this role had been lost, the coach continued to have a part to play in short haul, right up to the early twentieth century. In the end it was the rise of the motor car that finally killed it off.

The stagecoach is an important memory of the Old West, being the inspiration for a number of films and books, and playing an important role in many more. Its use spanned the entire nineteenth century, taking thousands of weary travellers along the bumpy roads.

Railroads

The railroads have played a vital role in American history, revolutionising the economy and allowing for easier settlement of the west. It began with the Baltimore and Ohio Railroad in 1828, which saw the start of a huge phase of construction, lasting until the economic downturn of 1873 in which many companies went bust. The Southern states tended to build shorter railways, usually linking cotton regions to ports and major settlements, and the absence of an interconnected rail network was a serious handicap during the Civil War. By contrast, in the North every major city was linked into a network by 1860, most of the lines owned by a couple of dozen operators.

Following the Baltimore and Ohio Railroad which opened to its first traffic in 1830, America closely watched the development of steam locomotion in Britain. Before long, railroads had replaced canals as the primary means of goods transport, and by the 1870s they had muscled out steam boats as well. Rail transport was vastly superior for a couple of reasons. Firstly they were able to operate all year round regardless of the weather conditions, whereas canals became unusable when the water froze. Secondly, the chance of a catastrophe occurring was far less; canal boats would occasionally sink whereas the chances of a train crashing were very low.

One of the key factors in deciding the Civil War was the successful use of the railroads by the North, whereas the South, with its far shorter lines and unconnected cities, was unable to move troops, goods and equipment as effectively. Most transport in the Confederacy was conducted via the rivers, which the Union was able to successfully blockade. After the war, a great deal of money was poured into the

Southern rail system as it was overhauled and expanded greatly, linking all the major cities together in the following years.

The Pacific Railway Acts were passed in 1862, allowing for the tracks to expand westward. The first transcontinental railroad was opened in 1869, allowing a journey from New York to San Francisco in six days. This was an absolute revolution in terms of travel, for it opened up the whole continent to new settlers and made the USA into a far more unified nation. Other transcontinental routes were opened in the south and along the Canadian border; to encourage people to start a new life in the west, farms and ranches were offered on credit. Meanwhile, goods such as wheat, cattle and minerals were transported back to the east. Between 1855 and 1871 the federal government operated a land grant system where new railroad companies in the west were given huge tracts of land that they could sell or pledge to bondholders. A staggering 129 million acres were granted in this way, followed by a further 51 million from the states. This enabled the opening of many new lines, particularly the Union Pacific-Central Pacific which offered fast services from San Francisco to Omaha and on to Chicago.

In 1873 a major economic downturn hit the USA, causing many railway companies to go bust. As a result of this, wages were cut for those still employed in the industry; this led to the great railroad strike of 1877 lasting for forty-five days and eventually requiring state and federal troops to break it up.

The railways play an important part in our image of the Old West, particularly in the time after the Civil War. The sense of adventure, of setting out for new lands at an incredible speed, lingers on to this day. Whereas pioneers of the previous generation had to undergo every hardship under the sun as they slogged their way west, the new breed of travellers simply journeyed for under a week on a train. The sheer ability of the average person to be able to visit different cities at will, without a huge amount of preparation, opened up the whole country and built up national feeling in an unprecedented way.

It was not unusual for people to gamble in order to pass the time on long journeys. Often a few travellers would come together and start up a game of poker. As they played some people would leave the game and others would join. By the time the train reached its final destination it was probable that none of the original players would be left, but the game would still be in progress, having taken on a life of its own.

The golden age of the Old West was also the golden age of rail transport. By the early decades of the twentieth century the automobile was pushing the train out of its dominant position, with paved roads meaning that trucks were now a viable option for goods transport and private motor cars being used for travel. By the middle of the century air travel was becoming the norm for long distance journeys. The railroad's day as the prominent method for transporting people to new frontiers is long over, but its central role in the development of America as we know it will never be forgotten.

Pony Express

Despite being a short-lived venture, the Pony Express (April 1860-October 1861) was a fast mail service which crossed the Great Plains, the Rocky Mountains and the High Sierras, running from St Joseph, Missouri to Sacramento, California. Preceding the rise of the telegraph as the dominant long distance message sender, it was the fastest means of communication between east and west and had the effect of tying California much closer to the Union on the eve of the Civil War. Messages were carried by riders in relays, to stations across the western United States. It reduced the time that it took to transfer mail from the east to west coasts to about ten days, far faster at the time than traditional delivery services.

Several men, including Alexander Majors, came up with the idea of the Pony Express, using a short route and mounted riders, at a time when stagecoaches were normally employed. The hope was to eventually win an exclusive government mail contract, though this never materialised. The actual cost of using the service was quite high at $5 for a half-ounce. The whole project was put together in just two months, with 120 riders, 400 horses and 184 stations. There were also several hundred personnel involved with the project, giving it perhaps the fastest setup time ever of such a grand project. A deeply religious man, Alexander Majors insisted that all of the riders took an oath promising not to use bad language, drink or gamble while working for his service. Anybody who broke these rules agreed to be released without pay.

The Pony Express showed that it was possible for a unified transcontinental system to be built and operated all the year round. Despite being eventually replaced by the telegraph, it remains part of the lore of the American West, largely thanks to its reliance on the skills and endurance of individual riders and horses. The telegraph turned out to be more practical, but could never match it in terms of spirit.

The stations were located about ten miles apart, all along the Express route. Ten miles was roughly the distance that a horse could travel at a gallop before tiring. At every station the rider would switch to a fresh horse, allowing him to always maintain high speeds. The rider would travel with nothing but the mail bag, a water sack, a Bible, a horn for letting the relay station master know to prepare the next horse, a revolver, and either a rifle or a second six-shooter. Eventually, everything except the mail bag, one revolver and a water sack was removed, making the horse even lighter and able to move slightly more quickly. The mail carriers themselves rode day and night and would change every hundred miles or so, though in emergencies it was not unknown for a rider to travel over two hundred miles in one go. Stations were sometimes built from scratch but were often put inside existing military forts or other structures.

As well as the hardship of travel, riders also had to face the possibility of attack from bandits or Native Americans. Because they did not travel with large amounts of money they were not especially targeted by highwaymen, but during the time the Express operated a war started with the Paiute tribe, and the Pony Express found itself targeted by raiders. As a result of this there were delays as sixteen employees were killed and many horses lost.

The riders had to be quite slim in order to avoid weighing down the horse, and most of them were teenage boys. Over its brief run, the Express had a number of riders who would later go on to become well known. William Cody, who would become Buffalo Bill, rode for a short time, as did Robert Haslam, who completed a record 380 mile trip during the middle of the Indian troubles. A rider named Jack Keetley managed to ride 340 miles in 31 hours, setting another record.

Despite its many successes, the Pony Express failed to gain the exclusive mail contacts that it had hoped for, and the enterprise was finally killed off by the start of the Civil War. Nonetheless it had been a remarkable undertaking which had involved huge numbers of people, horses and buildings. Simply to have set it up in the first place was a great achievement.

Pioneers' Wives

It is said that by 1869, the year the first transcontinental railroad was finished, over 350,000 pioneers had set out on the Oregon Trail, seeking to start a new life in a new land. Many of these were women with children, so whole families were often on the move. On the trail they would experience immense hardships and learn just how tough they really were. Although most women were accompanied by their husbands, some were single and made the trip alone, though this was quite rare. Groups of families would often form a wagon train for mutual protection and encouragement, and the sight of such a procession making its way through the wilderness is an iconic one.

Before a family could head west, the wagon had to be packed. This task fell normally to the women, who would have to carefully consider what to take with them. A list would be prepared, while household items that were no longer needed, or too big to be carried, would be sold off to help finance the trip. Clothes and furniture would be packed, but the main item that had to be taken care of was food. As much as possible would be brought with them, such as dried meat, perhaps a cow to be milked, beans, coffee, flour and salt. Many families would get into trouble and run low on food, and quite often they would be forced to slaughter some of the animals that they had with them. Furthermore, it was common to abandon items that had originally been thought of as essential, such as favorite pieces of furniture, as the extra weight became a burden.

As well as discarding furniture, there were often deaths on the journey, forcing loved ones to be buried in the wilderness. It was not uncommon for a child to fall out of a wagon and be run over, and other similar accidents often claimed lives.

Typhoid and cholera spread like wildfire through wagon trains, claiming many victims. There were also skirmishes with Natives, though this was a small risk compared to that of disease. Any children who were born on the trail would be forced to endure the roughest conditions and would not have a happy start to life; naturally enough, there was a high rate of infant mortality.

Upon arrival at their destination, even more work was needed as a house had to be built. In many cases the families would arrive in late summer or autumn, forcing them to build through the winter's cold. Women would soon learn how to use an axe and other tools and would work alongside their husbands a great deal of the time. As soon as spring arrived a garden would have to be planted, and this was a job which usually fell to the women. Trees would need to be removed and stumps cleared, and then the ground would need to be worked up. These were jobs which often required handling an ox or mule. Water would then need to be supplied for the garden, as well as for cooking, cleaning and washing. There were also the dangers posed by wild animals, and the occasional threat of Native attacks.

All in all, the decision to move west and start a new life was a momentous one, and was shared equally between husband and wife. The hardships encountered, both on the trail and upon arrival, would mark a person forever; yet modern America owes a lot to the brave people who were prepared to give up everything for the sake of a greater freedom, and who helped in the taming of the wild frontier lands.

Big Jack Davis

The train robbery is a staple of many western films and novels, and so it is interesting to consider who holds the dubious honour of being the earliest train robber in American history. Sometimes wrongly attributed to the James gang, the deed was actually first performed by Andrew Jackson Davis, known as Big Jack.

Davis (?-1877) began life as a miner in Nevada. Apparently a well-educated and highly intelligent man, he hoped to strike it rich and make a fortune, sharing a dream with countless others. When things began to grow tough for the miners he relocated to Gold Hill and opened a stable, attempting to start a new life as a businessman. For a while he slogged away at the difficult task of looking after horses, but after a time grew tired of it, sold the stable and bought a small mill near Virginia City. He continued legitimate business, providing services to the local community, but in secret he had already rounded up a gang of outlaws and was organising strikes against stagecoaches and wagons, using the mill to melt down stolen gold into usable bars.

Clearly Davis was a big thinker who probably would have gone a long way in life had he stayed on the right side of the law. However, he was busy hatching a bold new scheme and before long was putting it into action. On November 4th 1870, Davis and four accomplices boarded the Central Pacific Railroad train at Verdi and, on a pre-designated stretch of track in the middle of nowhere, slipped the pin of the express car, separating it from the passenger coaches. They entered the car, encountered no resistance, and took somewhere between $30,000-$40,000 in coins from the Wells Fargo operative. They then ordered the train to stop and rode away with their loot.

Although the plan had worked to perfection and nobody had been harmed, Davis was to be let down by one of his accomplices, R.A. Jones, who began to spend his share of the money wildly and probably started boasting about what he had done, especially after a few drinks. Before long he was taken into custody by the local sheriff and not only admitted his guilt but also named his fellow outlaws, leading to the arrests of everybody involved within a few days.

All five of the men received jail sentences and were sent to Nevada State Prison. Given ten years behind bars Davis became a model prisoner and refused to take part in an organised prison break in 1871. On this occasion twenty-nine inmates escaped, including three of his accomplices, though most were soon recaptured. Davis did not take the opportunity to flee, and even helped the authorities by providing information on the escapees. As a result of this he was considered for early parole and was released from prison on February 16th 1875.

After his release, Davis tried going straight for a time, but before long was back to robbing stagecoaches again, this time acting alone. He made it his policy to only hold up coaches with a single person riding shotgun, not wanting to risk getting into a big fire fight. Despite this his luck eventually ran out in 1877 when he attempted to rob a coach at Warm Springs, Nevada, and was shot dead in a brief gun battle.

Although much of the gold that Davis stole during the train robbery was later recovered, rumours persist that he buried a good part of it somewhere along the Truckee River, close to the scene of the hold-up. Whether or not this is true, his name will live on as the first man to successfully hold up a train and as the mastermind behind a truly daring, though ultimately unsuccessful, criminal scheme.

Geronimo

A prominent leader of the Chiricahua Apache, Geronimo (1829-1909) lived a long life which embraced both armed conflict and peaceful living. Born to the Bedonkohe group of the Apache, he was raised on land that was legally part of Mexico (modern day New Mexico in the United States) but which his family considered to belong to the Natives. It is said that his name came from his ferocity in battle, which caused the soldiers he was fighting to call on St Jerome (Geronimo) for protection.

He married at the age of seventeen, soon having three children. However, in 1858 a band of Mexican soldiers attacked his village while the men were away trading, and his mother, wife and children were all killed. As a result of this the Apache stepped up their raids on Mexican towns and villages, causing numerous casualties and throwing the whole region into a state of terror.

Geronimo became well known and respected among his own people for both his prowess in battle and for his 'spiritual' abilities, such as being able to walk without leaving tracks and to be able to survive gunshot wounds. He was also credited with telepathy. Though never actually a chief, he soon built up a large following and became a key war leader in the region. He married numerous times, often having several wives at once, occasionally losing them to the enemy or simply becoming bored with them and giving them up. From the late 1850s to the mid-1880s he fought countless battles against Mexican and US forces, often coming out on top despite being heavily outnumbered, and even making several daring escapes when cornered. During this time his reputation grew and grew, among both Natives and Whites. In the mid-1880s he led one of the last bands of independent

Indians in America, refusing to accept the government of the USA.

Being constantly harried by US forces and being utterly exhausted from the need to keep moving, Geronimo and his group of followers finally surrendered in 1886; he was sent as a prisoner to Fort Pickens but soon after was reunited with his family and moved several times. As time passed and he grew older, the public became willing to forgive the assaults that he had made upon them, and Geronimo became a major celebrity, being one of the last surviving great Native war leaders. He appeared at fairs and shows and was at the World's Fair in St Louis in 1904, selling pictures of himself and other souvenirs. The following year, when President Theodore Roosevelt was organising his inaugural parade, Geronimo was invited to ride with the procession, which he accepted.

Late in life Geronimo adopted Christianity, saying that he approved of its strong ethical teachings. For a time he was a member of the Dutch Reformed Church, but was eventually expelled as he refused to give up gambling; he remained a Christian but also continued to follow some of the old spirituality of his ancestors. Towards the end of his life he published an autobiography which was well received.

Geronimo finally died in 1909 at the age of seventy-nine, having been thrown from his horse and lying in the cold all night before being rescued. His life saw gigantic changes in Native living, as Indians were rounded up into reservations and the old ways of life collapsed. The world in which he died was utterly different to that into which he had been born.

American Civil War

The single bloodiest event in the history of America, the Civil War (1861-1865) was fought primarily over the issue of slavery and the rights of the individual states compared to the federal government. Eleven Southern slave states declared their secession from the USA, forming the Confederate States of America led by Jefferson Davies. They fought for independence against the Northern states, twenty of which had abolished slavery, while five still allowed it. These twenty-five states, collectively called the Union, had the advantage of a far superior population and industrial base. After four years of terrible and costly warfare, mostly fought in the South, the Confederacy was forced to surrender and slavery was outlawed across the nation. The Reconstruction era that followed, as matters arising from the war were settled and the ex-Confederacy states dealt with, caused issues that were not resolved for decades.

Events had really come to a head after the presidential election of 1860, in which the Republican Party was victorious, led by Abraham Lincoln. Although not favouring abolition of slavery at the time, the party was advocating banning the expansion of slavery beyond the states in which it already existed. However, many states in the South feared that this would be the tip of the iceberg which would lead to full abolition in the future; they felt that their way of life, which depending heavily on cotton plantations largely manned by slaves, was being threatened, and as a result seven states declared their secession as soon as the election result was known. Lincoln considered this to be an act of rebellion and it was only a matter of time before hostilities began.

The first shots were fired on April 12, 1861, when Confederate forces attacked a US military installation at Fort

Sumter. Lincoln immediately called for a volunteer army in each state to defend the Union. These events led to four more states siding with the Confederacy. An important early step by the Union was a naval blockade of the South, which virtually ended cotton exports upon which the rebels were heavily dependent. In September 1862 Lincoln made ending slavery into an official war goal, moving to a position of full emancipation.

The South managed some impressive military successes under commander Robert E. Lee, but in 1863 his northward advance was thrown back with heavy casualties at the Battle of Gettysburg. In the west, the Union gained control of the Mississippi River and managed to split the Confederacy in two. Over time the North was able to capitalise on its superiority in both numbers and industry, grinding down the South in battles of attrition. The war ended when Lee surrendered to Union General Ulysses S. Grant on April 9th, 1865.

The American Civil War was the earliest major industrial conflict, in which railroads, telegraph, steam ships and mass production were used effectively. The concept of Total War was developed, as was trench-based defence, which foreshadowed the Great War. The effect on the nation was colossal; around 620,000 soldiers died as well as vast numbers of the civilian population. It is estimated that ten percent of Northern males aged twenty to forty-five died in the conflict, while an immense thirty percent of white males aged eighteen to forty died in the South. The horror of this slaughter haunts America to the present day, and the fallout from the war was very important to the period of the Old West which followed it. People had become, to an extent, acclimatised to violence, and many of the most notorious gangs and outlaws had begun their careers as soldiers.

Texas Rangers

The Texas Ranger Division is a law enforcement agency with state-wide jurisdiction in Texas, based in the city of Austin. Their history dates back to 1823 when Stephen Austin employed ten men to act as rangers in order to protect new settlers who had arrived following the Mexican War of Independence. However, the organisation was not formally constituted until 1835, when Robert Williamson was chosen to be the first Major. Over the next two years the Rangers continued to grow.

Following the Texas Revolution (1835-1836) and the creation of the new Republic, President Mirabeau Lamar raised a force of over fifty Rangers to fight against the Cherokee and Comanche, partly because of the support that the Indians had given to Mexican troops. By the time Sam Houston became President in 1841 the number of Rangers had settled down to one hundred and fifty. Following numerous skirmishes with Native Americans, and after the annexation of Texas by the United States in 1846, several companies were mustered into Federal service to fight in the Mexican-American War. They acted as guides and guerrilla troops, establishing a reputation for fearlessness and ferocity, and played an important role in various battles. When Richard Addison Gillespie, a famous Ranger, died at the Battle of Monterrey he was held to have been so vital to US success that a nearby hill was named Mount Gillespie in his honour.

After the war ended, the Rangers were largely disbanded, but upon the election of a new Governor, Hardin Richard Runnels, the sum of $70,000 was allocated to fund a reworking of the force under John Salmon 'Rip' Ford, a Mexican War veteran. The size of the organisation was set at one hundred, and it took part in expeditions against the

Comanche and other tribes who had continued with their raids of settlers. Throughout the 1860s the Rangers mounted a series of successful campaigns and proved their great worth; Texas was such a huge state that the army could only provide thinly stretched and piecemeal support to the people living there, whereas with their greater experience the Rangers were able to respond far more effectively to the various threats, whether they were outlaws or Indians. Before long it was clear that a well-funded and organised force was essential to maintaining law and order.

Most Rangers fought for the Confederacy during the Civil War, and as a result the organisation was replaced by a Union-controlled version called the Texas State Police at the end of hostilities. However, this new version soon fell into disrepute and was disbanded after only three years. The year 1873 saw a new Governor, and once again the Rangers were reformed, quickly re-establishing themselves as a hugely successful peace-keeping force, killing or capturing several highly dangerous gunfighters as well as defeating the Comanche and Apache. They were also not without controversy, often using methods almost as brutal as that of their opponents, including intimidating and torturing captives to gain confessions and information. The service was heavily reformed in the early years of the twentieth century, and a complaints system was introduced to cut down on incidents of brutality.

The Rangers outlived the Old West and continue to this day, though the mystique of the late nineteenth century still lives on; a great deal of sensationalist books and even movies have portrayed the organisation, usually mixing fact with legend, and creating an interesting synthesis of myth and reality. Despite this there are many true tales of selflessness and bravery attached to the Rangers, and they have always been a potent force of law enforcement across the wide expanse of Texas.

Badges and Uniform of the Texas Rangers

Modern day Texas Rangers, in the same manner as their predecessors, do not have an actual prescribed uniform, though the State of Texas does provide guidelines as to what kind of clothing is suitable, stating that it must be 'western' in nature. Historically, Rangers wore whatever clothes they could find or afford, which were often ragged and worn out from heavy use. Although Rangers still acquire their own clothes today, they do receive an allowance to help pay for boots, gun-belts and hats.

As they were often carrying out missions on horseback, Rangers adapted their dress and personal attire to fit their needs. Throughout the nineteenth century the greatest influence was from the 'vaqueros', who were Mexican cowboys; saddles, spurs and ropes would tend to be modelled after those of the vaqueros, while most Rangers preferred to wear wide-brimmed sombreros rather than cowboy hats. They also favoured a square cut, knee-high boot with a high heel and pointed toes, in a more Spanish style. Both groups also tended to carry their guns in the same manner, with holsters positioned around their hips rather than low on the thighs; this made it easier to draw and shoot while riding a horse.

The wearing of badges only became common among the Texas Rangers in the late nineteenth century. The lack of regular badges until this point is usually put down to the nature of the work; there was simply not much to be gained by showing one to a desperate gunfighter or a hostile Indian. In addition, the pay tended to be quite low, so such a potentially expensive item was usually out of the question. Some Rangers did wear badges, however, with the earliest appearing around 1875. They were made locally and varied considerably from one another, but they were always in the shape of a star cut out from a Mexican silver coin (usually a five-peso piece), in a design reminiscent of the Texas lone star flag.

The current design of the Ranger badge, a star in a wheel, was adopted in 1962 when Ranger Hardy Purvis and his mother donated enough Mexican five-peso coins to provide badges for all sixty-two commissioned officers who were working at the time.

Wild Bill Hickok

One of the greatest legends of the Old West, James Butler Hickok (1837-1876) was born and raised in Illinois. Not a great deal is known about his early life, but it is clear that he was an excellent marksman from a very young age and practised shooting a good deal, especially with a pistol. His life of adventure started at the age of eighteen when he was involved in a fight with another young man, which resulted in both of them falling into a canal. Hickok mistakenly thought that he had killed his adversary and so fled the scene, moving to Kansas Territory. Upon arrival he joined General Jim Lane's 'Free State Army', which was actually an anti-slavery vigilante movement. In doing so he met a twelve-year-old William Cody, who would later go on to become Buffalo Bill.

It was also around this time that Hickok began calling himself Wild Bill, preferring it to his nickname of Duck Bill which he had been given by his fellow vigilantes. Leaving General Lane's force, he claimed a large area of land in Johnson Country, Illinois and was elected a constable of the nearby Monticello Township. In 1859 he joined the Russell, Majors and Waddell freight company, but after an incident in which he was injured by a bear he was sent to Nebraska to work as a stable hand while he recovered from his wounds.

In 1861 Hickok became involved in a dispute with the McCanles Gang, when David McCanles and some of his family and employees arrived at the station's office demanding money that they claimed they were owed. It is not certain exactly what happened next, but David McCanles was fatally shot, most probably by Wild Bill. Hickok and several others were tried for murder, but the judge ruled that they had acted in self-defence and so nobody was ever really held to account over the happenings. It is generally accepted that

Hickok was involved in a number of other fights, and killed several more men, during this period. He was known for being a dead-eye shot with a pistol, seeming never to miss.

During the Civil War Hickok performed a number of essentially unexciting roles, including that of a scout, and was mustered out in 1865. His fame began to grow in the same year after an incident in which he duelled one-on-one with a cowboy called Davis Tutt. After an argument over gambling debts, Tutt took Hickok's prized watch and said that he would not return it until Hickok paid him $45. Wild Bill claimed that he only owed $25 and therefore would not pay. The following day the two men met in the town square and fought a quick-draw pistol duel, the kind that is seen in numerous western films and novels, but in fact was actually very rare. In this instance both men fired at the same time, but Tutt missed whereas Hickok hit his opponent in the chest, killing him almost instantly. Once more he was charged with murder, later reduced to manslaughter, but was acquitted by the jury who decided that Tutt had been killed in a fair fight.

Shortly afterwards Hickok was interviewed by Harper's New Monthly Magazine, in which he talked about the fight and bragged about the hundreds of men that he claimed to have killed. He was already creating his own myth, and in fact it is probable that he had slain perhaps half a dozen enemies. He also claimed to have killed large numbers of Indians, but this too is likely to be a wild exaggeration.

In 1867 Hickok moved to Niagara Falls and acted in a stage play called 'The Daring Buffalo Hunters of the Plains'. This was not a great success, however, and before long he had given up acting, deciding to move into law enforcement. He ran for sheriff in Ellsworth County, Kansas, but came second and moved to the nearby town of Hays. By 1878 he was a deputy US Marshal and was involved in rounding up Union deserters. In September of that year he was slightly wounded in the foot while successfully rescuing a group of cattlemen who had been surrounded by Indians.

In 1869 Hickok was elected sheriff of Hays and city marshal of Ellis County, Kansas. Within a couple of months of beginning his job he had already killed two men, Bill Mulvey and Samuel Strawhun, in separate incidents in which they were disrupting the peace of the town. A jury was appointed to try the legality of these shootings, and found no irregularities. A year later he was almost killed in a saloon when attacked by two men. One of them pinned him to the ground while another put a gun to his head and pulled the trigger. The weapon misfired and Hickok grabbed his own guns, injuring one of his attackers and fatally wounding another.

Wild Bill failed to win re-election, but instead became marshal of Abilene, Kansas. Here he met, and ended up befriending, the outlaw John Wesley Hardin. During this period he shot and killed a saloon owner called Phil Coe. Hickok had been involved in a dispute with Coe for some time, and one day during a street brawl, which Wild Bill was doing his best to control, Coe fired two shots. Hickok ordered his arrest for discharging a firearm within the city limits. Coe initially claimed that he was only aiming at a dog, but then turned his gun on Hickok who immediately fired, leaving him fatally wounded. At the same moment a figure came round the corner, running towards the action, and instinctively Hickok turned and fired, to discover that, to his absolute horror, he had just shot down and killed one of his own deputies who was rushing to help him. As a result of this, Wild Bill was relieved of his duties soon after.

In 1873 he attempted acting once again, this time in a Buffalo Bill production called 'Scouts of the Plains', but was again unsuccessful. His eye sight began to deteriorate, as did his marksmanship, most probably as a result of trachoma. Always a heavy gambler, he was arrested several times for vagrancy and seems to have had a big problem holding on to money. In 1878 he married Agnes Lake, but soon left her and travelled with a wagon train towards South Dakota, hoping to find gold. On this journey he encountered Calamity Jane, who would later incorrectly claim to have been his wife.

Wild Bill finally met his end at Deadwood, after apparently having a premonition that this would be his final stop. While playing poker he was shot in the back of the head by Jack McCall and killed instantly. At the time he was holding a hand of cards consisting of two black Aces, two black Eights and a fifth, unknown card. Because of this, many years later it would become known as the 'dead man's hand.' McCall was later tried for murder and hung.

It is often hard to tell myth from reality when talking about Wild Bill Hickok, because his legend was being created in his own lifetime, both from his own words and those of the dime novelists who cashed in on his fame. Whatever the truth, Hickok remains as an iconic hero of the Old West.

George Custer

An iconic figure in American history, George Armstrong Custer (1839-1876) was a United States Army officer and cavalry commander, involved in both the Civil War and the Indian Wars. He is best remembered for his disastrous military campaign which culminated in the Battle of the Little Bighorn, commonly known as Custer's Last Stand.

Custer spent his early youth living with his half-sister and brother-in-law in Monroe, Michigan where he attended several schools. Following this, he enrolled in the United States Military Academy where he graduated in last place out of thirty-four candidates in June 1861. Despite his poor performance, he graduated just as the Civil War was beginning, meaning that the Union were desperate for officer recruits. This ensured that he was not doomed to a life of obscurity, as would probably have been the case had the nation been at peace. Made a second lieutenant, he saw action at the opening engagement of the war, the First Battle of Bull Run. Before long he had gained quite a reputation for bravery and was appointed to the rank of Captain, leading his men to capture the first Confederate battle flag of the war.

Continuing to see a great deal of action, Custer was eventually brought into the cavalry which he instantly took to. At the age of just twenty-three he was promoted to the rank of Brigadier General of Volunteers, making him one of the youngest ever men to hold such a high ranking position. He earned a reputation for recklessness, always leading his men into the thick of the fighting, but also was apt at careful planning, so that his aggressive charges were actually better coordinated than they looked. He married Elizabeth Bacon in 1864.

In June 1865, Custer took command of the 2nd Division of Cavalry, to march into Texas as part of the occupying force. During this period he encountered a near mutiny from the volunteer cavalry regiments who had been campaigning along the coast. Many of the men wanted to be mustered out of Federal service, but were instead forced to continue. They particularly resented the tough discipline and many considered Custer to be little more than a vain dandy. It is said that, having been mustered out at last, several of his former soldiers planned to ambush Custer and kill him, but he was warned about the trap and so avoided it.

Near the start of 1866 Custer was relieved of his volunteer work and returned to the rank of Captain in the 5th Cavalry. He took part in the developing Indian Wars and also dabbled in politics, considering running for Congress and taking part in debates over what the future should hold for the defeated Confederacy states. In such discussions he always advocated a mild approach that would allow the South to recover, both socially and economically. In 1873 he was sent to Dakota Territory to protect a railroad survey against the Lakota, clashing for the first time with this nation. In 1874, Custer led an expedition into the Black Hills and announced the discovery of gold on French Creek. Custer's announcement triggered the Black Hills Gold Rush. Among the towns that immediately grew up was Deadwood, South Dakota, notorious for lawlessness.

The expedition went into a region with incredibly high tensions between Natives and settlers. Americans continually broke treaty agreements and advanced further westward, resulting in violence and acts of depredation by both sides. To take possession of the Black Hills (and thus the gold deposits which had been found there), and to stop Indian attacks, the U.S. decided to corral all remaining free plains Indians. The 7th Cavalry departed from Fort Lincoln on May 17, 1876, part of a larger army force planning to round up remaining free Indians. Meanwhile, in the spring and summer of 1876, the Lakota holy man Sitting Bull had called together the largest ever gathering of plains Indians to discuss what to do about the whites. It was this united encampment of Lakota, Northern Cheyenne, and Arapaho Indians that the 7th met at the Battle of the Little Bighorn.

What exactly occurred before the battle is uncertain, but Custer divided his men into three divisions, thus ensuring that they would all be hugely outnumbered. The battle quickly turned into a rout as the US forces were overcome by wave after wave of Native attacks. Custer died fighting alongside his troops, his death quickly becoming something of a legend. Every single one of his men was slain.

It is probable that Custer had designs on a glittering career in politics, and it has been suggested that he was even considering running for President one day. Wanting all the glory for himself, he led his men into an impossible situation. It is a fitting testament that he is remembered today more for his death than for his life.

Crazy Horse

A war leader of the Oglala Lakota, Crazy Horse (1840?-1877) lived during a period in which native ways of life were being swiftly eradicated, and tensions were high between whites and Indians. He fought in numerous battles, including the action at Little Bighorn, and remains an iconic Native American. His year of birth is uncertain, but is most probably around 1840.

How Crazy Horse came by his name is not known for sure. His father may have given it to him, having the same name himself, or he may have acquired it via a vision. What is certain though is that he grew up in violent times; in 1854 he was involved in the Grattan massacre in which his village was attacked by a small detachment of the US army, with the eventual result of all the soldiers being killed.

Crazy Horse soon began to experience visions, and went with his father to undergo a vision quest. In his trance, he found himself taken to the south, the traditional region of death, and then to the west where he was given a medicine bundle to protect him and told that he would lead a long life and be the protector of his people. He was also shown how he should paint his face for battle (most notably a yellow lightning bolt down the left side) and was given a sacred song.

By the 1860s Crazy Horse was becoming well known for his skill in battles, most of which were fought against other Native American nations of the Great Plains. In 1866, he was one of a small band who decoyed a group of the US army, leading to the Fetterman massacre in which, once again, every single soldier was killed. However he was not always on the victorious side; the following year he was involved with the Wagon Box Fight, in which over one thousand Natives attacked a wood cutting crew near Fort Kearny. The crew fled to a circle of wagon boxes (wagons with no wheels) which they used as cover. The Lakota waited until the soldiers had fired and then charged, expecting there to be a significant delay while they reloaded. However, the soldiers were equipped with new breach loading rifles which could fire ten rounds per minute, compared with only three per minute for the old muzzle loaders. As a result of this the Lakota took heavy losses and were forced to withdraw.

Crazy Horse took three wives, though had only one child, a daughter who died young. His first wife, Black Buffalo Woman, caused controversy as she was with Crazy Horse when still married to her first husband, No Water. As a result of this No Water almost killed Crazy Horse, firing at him with a pistol but only managing to wound him in the jaw. The matter was later settled without further bloodshed.

In 1876 Crazy Horse led a large band of Lakota and Cheyenne in the Battle of the Rosebud, one of the conflicts leading up to Little Bighorn which occurred a week later. On this occasion Custer and his 7th Cavalry were wiped out, though the role of Crazy Horse in this battle is not known for sure. It seems certain that he was a major figure however, and several accounts tell of his bravery in action. Following this he led his troops in action in two more engagements at Slim Buttes and Wolf Mountain, but on these occasions was unsuccessful, suffering heavy losses.

Eventually, with his people dying from malnutrition and cold, Crazy Horse decided to surrender and settled in the Red Cloud Agency. Although remaining at peace, there was still a great deal of mistrust between the Natives and their captors, and eventually it was decided that Crazy Horse had to be arrested. In the course of the arrest he attempted to break free and was stabbed with a bayonet, dying a few hours later, probably aged around thirty-six.

Although he had not had the long life which his vision quest seemed to promise, Crazy Horse is well remembered today and so has lived on in a sense. His sacred song, which he received in his youth, is still sung to this day by the Oglala people.

Gunfight 'at the O.K. Corral'

A fine example of a mixture of fantasy and reality, this legendary gun battle did not even take place at the O.K. Corral, but actually on Fremont Street in the town of Tombstone. It only lasted about thirty seconds, though in this time three men were killed and several others wounded. It is generally held to be the most famous gun fight of the Old West and symbolises the struggle between law enforcers and outlaws, during an era in which law and order were often haphazard affairs with few officers around to enforce the peace. Despite its modern day status as an event of which virtually everybody has heard, it was not actually widely known to the public before the 1931 publication of a book entitled 'Wyatt Earp: Frontier Marshal', published two years after Earp's death. A number of movies followed, most notably one in 1957 entitled 'Gunfight at the O.K. Corral', after which the name stuck. Since then, various books and films have described the conflict, though with a very wide range of accuracy.

Tombstone was, at the time, something of a frontier boom town with a great deal of activity, including mining. Virgil Earp was the town's Marshal, as well as being Deputy US Marshal for the region. He had a policy of protecting the interests of businessmen and those directly involved with the town, as opposed to the cowboys who sometimes passed through. This was in direct contrast to the County Sheriff who tended to support the cowboys, even though they were seen as being little more than outlaws by a large part of the population.

On 25th June, 1880, Virgil led a party which tracked down six US army mules which had been stolen from a nearby ranch, eventually finding them at the McLaury ranch, catching the thieves in the act of re-branding the animals. The cowboys said that they would return the mules, which the lawmen accepted in order to avoid bloodshed; however, this promise was never followed through. The main culprits were Frank and Tom McLaury and associates Ike and Billy Clanton. Following these events some handbills were printed describing the crime and naming the thieves, and this caused Frank McLaury to publicly threaten to kill Virgil.

In 1881 a stagecoach driver and a passenger were killed during a robbery carried out by local cowboys, and Virgil's brother, Wyatt Earp (who was hoping to run for County Sheriff), attempted to bargain with Ike to hand over those who were responsible. These talks broke down and Ike began threatening Wyatt, claiming that he was trying to undermine his position with local cowboys. Soon afterwards Virgil arrested two cowboys who were thought to have robbed another stagecoach, and this convinced Ike that the law enforcers were out to get him, causing even more threats to be issued. Over time matters went downhill further and there were several encounters in town between the rival factions. Eventually, after Virgil and Wyatt had pistol-whipped some of the cowboys for being illegally armed, things came to a head. Five of the clan (Frank and Tom McLaury, Ike and Billy Clanton and friend Billy Claiborne) and four lawmen (Wyatt, Virgil and Morgan Earp along with their friend Doc Holliday) confronted each other on Fremont Street, near the entrance to the O.K. Corral and within a few moments fighting broke out.

In thirty seconds about thirty shots were fired at very close range. Ike Clanton and Billy Claiborne ran away unharmed, Frank and Tom McLaury and Billy Clanton were killed. Meanwhile Virgil and Morgan Earp and Doc Holliday were wounded but survived, and Wyatt Earp was unharmed. The violence did not end with the fight however, as following their acquittal for murder, the Earp brothers found themselves the target of a vendetta by Ike and his friends. This led to a series of attacks and counter attacks which has sometimes been described as a small war.

Although certainly a dramatic event, the shootout is really more of a tragedy as it shows how utterly unable the two sides were to reconcile their differences, and was therefore a bloody outcome of a bloody age. Not well known at the time, the fight is now one of the most important quasi-legends of the Old West, showing the importance of film and literature in creating our modern sense of history.

Robert Clay Allison

Although not among the first rank in heroes or villains of the Old West, Robert Clay Allison (1840-1887) was a gunfighter, known for his dangerous temper and wild mood swings. Working on the family farm until he was twenty-one, Allison joined the Confederate army on the outbreak of the Civil War, serving with the Tennessee Light Artillery. He soon received a medical discharge, the reason for this was stated as being an old head injury that caused him to have massive swings of mood. Later, he joined the cavalry and served until his force surrendered at the end of the war, being held as a POW for a few days.

Moving around the southern states, Allison (known most of the time as Clay) began to be noted as a dangerous man, drinking and gambling heavily and generally running amuck. He would ride with local cowboys down the main streets of towns, firing his guns at lamps. Towards the end of 1870 he was involved in an incident in which a group of men broke into a jail and abducted a man who was being held on suspicion of murder. Clay tied the man behind his horse and rode fast until he was dead, then cut his head off.

In 1874, Clay killed a gunman called Chunk Colbert, gunning him down while eating with him in a saloon. Colbert had been involved in a long running quarrel with his foe, but the two still sat down to eat dinner together. At a certain point in the meal Colbert drew his gun and tried to shoot his opponent, but his weapon jammed against the table and Clay shot him in the head, killing him instantly. According to witnesses, when asked why he had gone to dinner with a man who intended to kill him, Clay said that he did not want to send a man to Hell on an empty stomach. A year later he led a lynch mob in hanging a local suspected murderer. When confronted by the victim's family he ended up shooting it out with them, slaying another man in the process. Although arrested for murder, the killing was ruled justifiable as self-defence.

The following year Clay and his brother John ended up in a shootout with a local sheriff and two deputies following a dispute over whether or not they were to hand over their guns upon entering the town. John was badly wounded but Clay gunned down the sheriff, upon which the deputies fled. Once again he was arrested and this time charged with manslaughter, but yet again the charges were dropped. This incident led to him becoming fairly famous and made people take notice of him.

In 1877 Clay sold the ranch that he had been working to his brother John and moved to Missouri, then to Dodge City in Kansas. At this time famed law enforcer Wyatt Earp was deputy marshal of the region, and legend goes that he was involved in a stand-off with Clay, in which the gunfighter eventually surrendered his arms. Whether or not this is true, it is certain that Allison had quite a reputation by this time, even in somewhere as rough as Dodge.

In the early 1880s Clay put more of his time into ranching, working with two of his brothers; he also married, eventually having two daughters. For all his wild days and shootouts, in the end he died in a simple accident in 1887. He fell from a cart and was crushed by one of the wheels. A marker on his grave reads: "He never killed a man that did not need killing".

Buffalo Bill

Famous both in his own time and today, William Cody (1846-1917) was as important as novelists such as Ned Buntline in creating the myths and legends of the Old West, mixing truth and fantasy in his portrayal of the dangerous frontier. He took the name Buffalo Bill after hunting down huge numbers of buffalo in the late 1860s on a contract to supply the Kansas Pacific Railroad with meat.

Born to Quaker parents, Cody's early life was dominated by his father Isaac's strong anti-slavery views. Not a man to mince his words, Isaac Cody gave speeches and often enraged his audiences which were full of slave owners. In one notorious incident he was actually stabbed by a mob of pro-slavery agitators and never fully recovered from his wound. On another occasion a group of his enemies planned to kill him as he rode home to visit his family, but William learned of the scheme and rode thirty miles to warn his father, most probably saving his life. Despite this, Isaac died in 1857 and William went to work for a wagon train. His job involved riding up and down the length of the train, delivering messages. After this, and still in his early teens, he joined up unofficially as a scout with the army, which was on its way to Utah to put down a supposed (but false) Mormon rebellion. Cody later claimed to have killed his first Indian during this time. Before long he had decided to head off to search for gold, but this scheme evaporated when he was offered a position riding for the Pony Express. He stayed with the Express until he was suddenly called home to attend to his sick mother.

His mother did not die, and as soon as he was old enough Cody enlisted in the cavalry, but was discharged after a few years. He drifted through a number of different jobs, including the above-mentioned buffalo hunting contract. Most notably in this period of his life, he received the Medal of Honour in 1872, awarded for 'gallantry in action' while serving as a scout. During these years he was noted for his bravery in combat, especially in the numerous skirmishes against Native Americans that occurred. By his mid-twenties he had seen a great deal of military action and had a ready supply of stories to tell.

Towards the end of 1872, Cody moved to Chicago to join his friend Texas Jack Omohundro in performing a stage show called 'Scouts of the Prairie', produced by dime novelist Ned Buntline. Finding that the theatrical life suited him, Cody wrote a new production called 'Scouts of the Plains' and successfully encouraged his friend Wild Bill Hickok to come and join him. Although Wild Bill did not take to performing, the show was a triumph. It toured for ten years, changing greatly over time, and in 1883 a new production, 'Buffalo Bill's Wild West' was founded, touring annually. The show travelled all over America and even went to Europe, greatly increasing Cody's fame.

By 1893 the title of the performance had been changed to 'Buffalo Bill's Wild West and Congress of Rough Riders of the World', beginning with a horseback parade with groups representing diverse cultures, from United States Cavalry to Native American, to Asian. Sitting Bull appeared with a group of twenty braves, and Annie Oakley would often take part, giving sharpshooting exhibitions. An essential part of the performance was the recreation of attacks on settlers by Native Americans, with the Indians being driven off by the timely arrival of reinforcements of cowboys or cavalry. Many of the perceptions of the Old West that surface in films and novels were inspired by these shows, with the Native Americans always being defeated in the end.

In 1887 the show went to England as part of the Jubilee celebrations for Queen Victoria. It played in London, Birmingham and Salford and was generally well received, sparking considerable interest in the Wild West in Britain. This was followed by a European tour in which Cody met the

Pope. By 1893 the show was back in America and playing next to the Chicago World's Fair. Cody was not given permission to play at the Fair, so set up just outside it and drew many of the crowds away. Many years later he teamed up with Pawnee Bill and together they created the 'Two Bill's' show, which was forced to close due to financial problems. In 1879 he published a well-received autobiography.

Throughout his life, Cody was involved in projects outside of his theatrical work, including a failed attempt to move into the business of irrigation. He founded the town of Cody in north Wyoming, and opened a hotel there. He also set up a nearby ranch and branded his own cattle. Active till late in life, he finally died at the age of seventy, in Denver.

Perhaps the greatest superstar of the Old West, Cody brought to the stage numerous genuine adventurers, ranging from Native Chiefs to renowned lawmen and sharpshooters. Rather than hiring actors to play the parts of his heroes, he was able to attract the heroes themselves to play their own parts, and thus created an enduring legacy which has easily lasted to this day.

Jesse James

An outlaw, bank and train robber, murderer and gang leader, Jesse James (1847-1882) was the most famous member of the James-Younger gang and a celebrity within his own lifetime. Born in Clay County, Missouri, he had an older brother called Frank, and a younger sister. His father was a hemp farmer and Baptist minister who was doing rather well in life, owning both land and slaves. However, during the gold rush he moved to California to minister to those who had travelled there in search of riches, and died when Jesse was only three years old. His widow remarried twice and had several more children.

The Civil War most probably had a formative effect on the young Jesse, as the region dissolved into bitter guerrilla style fighting, with both sides committing atrocities against each other. Taking the Confederate side, the family found themselves on the losing end, and Frank joined a company of men who made guerrilla attacks on Union forces. At one point the family farmhouse was raided by Northern troops who abused the children in the hope of being told where Frank was hiding; they were unable to catch him though, and it is likely that he was involved in a large scale massacre of anti-slavery activists. At the start of 1864, Jesse joined his brother and they fought together, being witness to and part of the terrible deeds of the Civil war which involved killing civilians and any troops who tried to surrender. Along the way, Frank lost his arm to a shotgun blast and Jesse was shot in the chest and almost killed.

Following the defeat of the Confederacy the atmosphere in Missouri hardly improved and there was still widespread violence between both individuals and armed groups of veterans. It is possible that Frank and Jesse took part in, but did not lead, a bank robbery in 1866; certainly ex-Confederate troops were involved led by Archie Clement, who had organised guerrilla activities with a band of men during the war. Shortly afterwards Clement was shot dead by the local militia. The remains of the group, possibly including the James brothers, continued to conduct raids on banks for the next couple of years, though their numbers soon dwindled as men were killed or arrested.

In 1869 Jesse began to grow famous after robbing a bank in which he killed the cashier. He and Frank made a daring escape afterwards which captured the imagination of the war-shocked region and made him into something of an anti-hero celebrity. This resulted in him being officially labelled as an outlaw and a reward placed on his capture. Soon afterwards the brothers joined with a man called Cole Younger and his three brothers, along with a number of other ex-Confederates, in what became known as the James-Younger gang. They robbed banks and stagecoaches and even a fair, often in front of large crowds, and seemed to take as much pleasure in putting on a public performance as in getting away with the money. Naturally enough, this made them even more famous. By 1873 they had turned to train robbery, though seldom took any money off the passengers, preferring to go for the safe.

Because of the train hold-ups, the Pinkerton Detective Agency was hired to bring down the gang. After a number of agents were killed Allan Pinkerton, the founder of the Agency, took up the case as a personal vendetta. On January 25th 1875, detectives carried out a raid on the James farm and threw in an incendiary device, killing Jesse's young half-brother and blowing one of his mother's arms off. Although they later denied it, it is generally thought that the intent was to burn the farm down entirely. As a result of this there was suddenly a good deal of sympathy for the gang, and a bill was actually proposed in the Missouri State Legislature offering amnesty, which was only narrowly defeated. Stories began to circulate which painted Jesse as a kind of Robin Hood figure, though in reality he never shared any of his takings outside of the gang.

In September 1876, the group made a botched attempt to rob a bank in Northfield, Minnesota. The cashier refused to open the safe and the townsfolk realised what was happening and started returning fire with the outlaws. The gang managed to escape but left two behind dead, and virtually every man was wounded. Jesse and Frank split from their comrades after this, going their own way.

The two brothers spent a while living incognito, but before long Jesse had rounded up a new gang and was carrying out robberies once again, though Frank seems to have wanted to settle down and took no further part in his adventures. The new group had far less experience than the James-Younger boys, and before long was falling apart. Around this time Jesse rented a house in Missouri, near to where he was born. He took up with Robert and Charley Ford, a pair of brothers with whom he hoped to be able to conduct robberies. However, aiming to gain the reward money for his capture, Robert shot Jesse in the back of the head, killing him instantly. It is likely that the Governor of Missouri knew in advance or at least approved of the slaying; although sentenced to death for murder the Ford brothers were given a full pardon within two hours and set free.

The cowardly manner in which Jesse was slain only added to his reputation and reinforced the Robin Hood image which he had built. In actual fact, despite the somewhat cartoon nature of some of his crimes, he was a hardened outlaw who probably killed dozens of people in his day, making his eventual demise almost fitting.

Belle Starr

Born Myra Maybelle Shirley, and known to her family as May, Belle Starr (1848-1889) was born on a farm near Carthage, Missouri. Her father, John, gave up farming in the 1860s, selling his land and moving the family into Carthage to work as the owner of an inn and livery stable. From a young age Belle was immersed in the rivalries and tensions of the Old West. Her mother was from the Hatfield clan who were at the time fighting a bitter war against their rivals, the McCoys, which would become a legend in its own right. Furthermore, while growing up she was friends with Jesse James and the Younger Brothers who would one day turn to crime and form their own criminal gangs.

Belle received a fine education, graduating from Carthage Female Academy, but during the Civil War the family were forced to move to Texas after Union attacks on Carthage. Here Belle reacquainted herself with the James and Younger clans while her brother John served with them, fighting for the Confederacy. After the war, Jim Reed moved to Texas. He and Belle were old childhood friends and they were soon married. Their daughter Rosie was born in 1868 (though was rumoured to actually be Cole Younger's daughter) and was followed by a son, James, born in 1871. Belle began to perfect her image, riding side-saddle, dressed in a black velvet riding suit and carrying two loaded pistols.

Jim Reed began married life honestly enough, attempting to earn a living through farming. Before long, however, he turned to crime, falling in with the Starr gang, a Cherokee Indian group involved with cattle and horse theft. In 1869 he shot a man down, claiming that his victim had shot his brother, and was forced to flee to California with his family. Two years later he returned to Texas after being in trouble with the law once again, this time for counterfeiting money. Towards the end of 1873 Jim, along with a couple of accomplices, robbed a wealthy Native of around thirty thousand dollars' worth of gold coins. Belle may or may not have been involved with the robbery, but she was named as an accessory and forced to hide out with her children while Jim went his own way. Apparently, at this point in her life she began to behave wildly, spending much time in saloons drinking, gambling and causing quite a sensation by firing off her guns in the street. These accounts could well be exaggerated but most probably contain a core of truth.

Meanwhile Jim Reed's luck was about to run out. After robbing a stagecoach he went on the run again, but was tracked down and shot in Paris, Texas, as he attempted to escape from the law. Now a widow, Belle put her children into the care of relatives and took up full time with the Starr clan in Arkansas. She played a key role in the gang's doings, organising and planning their outlaw activities and harbouring those wanted by the state. She made large amounts of money, and through a mixture of bribery and seduction was able to keep the law at arm's length and ensure that her comrades were seldom charged, even when arrested. In 1880 she married Samuel Starr, a member of the gang.

In 1882 Belle and Samuel were finally brought to justice over a charge of horse stealing, found guilty and sentenced to a year in prison each. Belle served nine months of her sentence, apparently a model prisoner; however, she did not change her ways and as soon as they were released she and Samuel returned to the Indian Territory and continued to be outlaws. Over the following years she was arrested several more times for one thing and another, but was always released for lack of evidence. She lost her second husband in 1886 when he was murdered by a long-term enemy. Following this, Belle took a number of lovers and continued to organise the outlaws.

Her death occurred on February 3rd, 1889, when she was shot in the back, while riding, by an unknown assailant. The mystery of who gunned down Belle Starr will never be solved, but her violent death only added to her reputation and increased her legendary status.

Much fact and fiction has been written about Belle Starr and, as with many famous faces of the Old West, it is sometimes difficult to tell the myth from the reality. What is certain however, is that she had a remarkable and dangerous career and was the inspiration for a whole swath of popular books and, later, movies.

Pinkerton Men

The Pinkerton National Defence Agency was founded in the 1850s as a security and private detective organisation. It shot to fame in the Civil War when Abraham Lincoln used Pinkerton detectives as his personal bodyguard. Despite its ultimate failure to protect Lincoln it nevertheless grew into a vast organisation, even rivalling the US army in size, and as a result was actually banned in Ohio for fear that it was growing too powerful. During the labour disputes of the latter half of the nineteenth century, Pinkerton agents were used to infiltrate unions and to aid in breaking up strikes, and therefore acquired quite a reputation as a fearsome adversary to united labour.

The organisation has its origins in the 1850s when Allan Pinkerton and attorney Edward Rucker formed the North-Western Police Agency, soon renamed the Pinkerton Agency. Operating out of Chicago, it quickly became popular with certain employers who turned to the new organisation to aid them with troublesome workers and organised labour.

From the early 1870s the newly formed Department of Justice contracted out work to the Pinkerton Agency, asking them to track down criminals who were guilty of breaching federal law. Up until this point in time, long before the formation of the FBI, federal laws were hard to enforce, and so the Pinkerton agents took on this very important role with some success. Despite this, crossover between the Agency and the US government was frowned upon, and in 1893 a law was passed banning members of the Agency from being employed by the government.

Franklin Gowen, president of the Philadelphia and Reading Railroad, hired the agency to infiltrate the labour unions that were operating in the company's mines. Agent

James McParland worked his way into the trust of the Molly Maguires, a radical secret working class organisation. Because of the evidence that he collected, the rail bosses were able to topple the Maguires with a series of sensational arrests and trials, and the whole experience boosted the status of the Pinkertons quite dramatically.

In July 1892, a vicious labour dispute took place involving steel workers, named the Homestead Strike. Three hundred Pinkerton men were called in, their job being to protect the mill from harm, and to ensure the safety of the replacement workers from the strikers. During the day of July 6th, seven Pinkerton agents and nine rioters were killed in the rioting. Eventually the state militia had to be called out to restore order.

Three years later the Agency received positive notice, when agent Frank Geyer tracked down serial killer H.H. Holmes. Holmes had murdered a huge number of people in Chicago during the World Fair of 1893, possibly as many as two hundred and fifty, though he was only charged with a handful. Possibly America's first serial killer, the capture of Holmes was a big achievement, and one about which Geyer would later write a book.

Throughout the time of the Old West, Pinkerton agents were hired to track down various famous outlaws such as Jesse James, the Wild Bunch (including Butch Cassidy and the Sundance Kid) and the Reno Gang. In 1874 two agents were involved in a shootout with the Younger brothers, in which one of the Pinkerton men was killed along with a couple of members of the gang. The Agency was also often hired as security for the transport of large amounts of money and valuables. As such they often found themselves fighting outlaws, and therefore tended to be heavily armed.

The Pinkerton Agency outlasted all of the characters of the Old West and continues today, albeit in a heavily modernised form. During the nineteen-thirties it moved away from its role in infiltrating labour movements, but during its formative years in the late nineteenth and early twentieth century it was commonly regarded as the enemy of organised labour and often as a tool of wealthy capitalists.

Bill Longley

A gunfighter and outlaw, William Longley (1851-1878) was as ruthless and as quick to draw as they come. Growing up on a farm in Texas as the Civil War drew to a close, he found himself part of a culture of resentment, as the state was under the control of victorious Union forces. Having received a decent education, he suddenly dropped out of school and began to live a wild life, drinking, gambling and womanising.

His criminal career began in 1868 when he and two accomplices encountered three freed slaves who were riding through town. They attempted to force the men at gunpoint to descend into a dry creek bed, and when one tried to escape Longley shot him dead. In the chaos of the post war years, the outlaws were never brought to justice for this killing.

By 1869 Longley had taken up with his brother-in-law, John Wilson, and the two went on a rampage around the state, robbing and assaulting people and killing at least one freed slave, and quite possibly more. Finally their activities aroused the attention of the law-enforcers, and a reward of $1000 was offered for their capture. At some point, Wilson was killed, possibly by other outlaws, and Longley fled Texas to avoid arrest.

Moving north, he enlisted in the cavalry, but the tough military discipline did not appeal to him and he deserted, only to be recaptured and sentenced to two years hard labour at court martial. After serving four months he was allowed to rejoin his regiment and made more of a go of things, being noted for his ability as a marksman. However, he eventually deserted again in 1872, this time getting clean away.

After spending some time drifting, Longley returned to Texas by 1873 where he was promptly accused of murdering another freed slave. This time he was captured by a local sheriff who intended to collect a reward for his arrest, but when the reward was not granted he allowed his captive to go free. It is also possible that Longley's uncle paid a bribe to get his nephew out of trouble.

Moving rapidly from place to place, and becoming increasingly out of control, Longley committed several more murders, including those of several friends. A new bounty was placed on his head but he managed to keep one step ahead of the lawmen and even shot down a rival outlaw, Lou Shroyer. Eventually he attempted to settle down to farming and rented some land from a local preacher, William Lay. Before long, however, he had been in a fight with his landlord's nephew and found himself jailed. As soon as he was released he rode to Lay's farm and shot the preacher dead, blaming him for his imprisonment. Afterwards, Longley broke some friends out of jail and escaped to Louisiana.

Even during this violent time in American history, such a string of murders were bound to catch up with him in the end, and indeed Bill Longley was eventually surrounded by an armed posse and taken back to Texas. He was tried on one charge of murder, found guilty, and hung on October 11, 1878.

Long after his death, rumours began circulating that Longley had actually survived the execution and was still alive, these tales being started by his father. The story of his survival held such weight, even into the twenty-first century, that in 2001 his remains were exhumed, and it was confirmed that Bill Longley did indeed lie in his marked grave.

Really he should not be considered a gunfighter but rather a simple murderer as most of his victims were unarmed, and he is only known to have been involved in one actual gunfight. He was a character who seemed to place absolutely no value on human life, an extreme product even by the standards of his own times. In total he claimed to have killed thirty-two people, and it is quite possible that this is not too much of an exaggeration.

Sam Bass

A successful, though little remembered outlaw, Sam Bass (1851-1878) did not have an easy start to life. His parents were both dead by the time he was ten, and he and his siblings ended up living with an uncle who was violent and abusive. At the age of eighteen he left home and drifted for a while, before moving to Denton, Texas, in 1871.

Bass attempted to live as an honest man and tried out several business enterprises. It was the failure of these schemes that led him towards a career in crime, and before long he was founding his own criminal gang. On September 18th 1877, he held up a Union Pacific railroad which was carrying gold, and made off with around $60,000. This was, and remains today, the largest amount ever stolen from a Union Pacific train.

Having escaped justice, the gang became increasingly confident and carried out numerous robberies, usually netting fairly small to medium amounts on each hit. On one notorious day in 1878 they held up two coaches and four trains within a twenty-four hour period near to Dallas, and attracted the attention of both the Texas Rangers and the Pinkerton Detective Agency.

Bass was able to avoid running into the lawmen for some time, but eventually he was betrayed by one of his associates, which allowed an ambush to be set up. On 19th July 1878, as the gang were scouting the area for their next robbery they were noticed by a local sheriff who attempted to disarm them. In the ensuing chaos the sheriff was shot dead and Bass attempted to flee. However, as he ran he was shot down by two Texas Rangers, who had been waiting to ambush him, and badly hurt. Taken into custody, he died from his wounds the next day.

Whether Bass would have 'turned bad' had he received a more normal childhood is a question that is interesting to ask but impossible to answer. His life story does show how strongly the lure of 'easy' money was to young men at the time, and in many ways the story of Bass could be the story of a good many outlaws, who simply did not fit into normal society and so turned to crime as a way to live.

Doc Carver

A sharpshooter and general showman, William Frank Carver (1851-1927) was born in Winslow, Illinois. Virtually nothing is known about his early life, though he would later tell many tall stories of supposed exploits from his youth. The nickname 'Doc' was due to the fact that as a young man he had a habit of rescuing small animals which had been injured and nursing them back to health. As a result of this his father gave him the nickname 'little doc', and as he grew older he dropped the 'little'. He was also trained as a dentist and practised as such for some time.

Moving around the West, he encountered Buffalo Bill and other important figures of the time. It was while travelling in Nebraska that he began to seriously practise with firearms, finding that he had considerable natural skill in this area. Perhaps part of the reason that he took to training with a gun was because of the unstable nature of the frontier at this time; there was still simmering tension between settlers and Native Americans where trouble could begin at any moment. Carver seems to have been particularly good with a rifle, and is mentioned as being a marksman in Buffalo Bill's 1879 autobiography.

In 1876 Carver moved to California and began to offer a challenge to interested parties. Using the name 'Evil Spirit', which he claimed had been given to him by a Native chief, he would use a machine to throw glass balls into the air. He would fire at them using a rifle, while his opponent would use a shotgun, thus having a much easier shot. Another version of this challenge involved Carver shooting from horseback while his opponent was allowed to stand. In 1878 he won a shooting competition and was named as Champion Rifle Shot of the World. It was claimed by the papers that he could put a rifle bullet through a silver coin as it was thrown into the air. He added to his own legend by publishing an autobiography that was in fact almost totally fictionalised. In the same year, 1878, he married.

Carver's great dream was to shoot and win against world renowned trap shooter Captain Adam Bogardus, whose talents he greatly admired. Despite this, Bogardus refused to even reply to his challenges, and Carver set off on a European tour, showing off his skills with pistol, rifle and shotgun. Upon his return to America Bogardus finally agreed to a match, and Carver just edged victory. As a result of his defeat, Bogardus suddenly became very keen on a rematch, and the two shot it out many more times on a tour, with Carver winning the vast majority of the encounters.

In the early 1880s, Carver teamed up with Buffalo Bill in a new Wild West show, and gave exhibitions of sharp shooting, often joined by Bogardus. The performances were very successful, but Bill and Carver did not get on personally and so went their own ways at the end of the first season. Carver set up his own Wild West show and directly challenged Bill's dominance of the market. However, he was unable to usurp his former friend's status as America's leading showman, and eventually shut his version of the show down. Following this disappointment he continued to appear in various performances, showing off his sharpshooting skills

Eventually, towards the end of the decade, Carver designed a new show called Wild America, which toured around America and Europe, and even went as far as Australia where it met with great success. Despite this he had difficulty in handling the finances of the operation, and the show broke up after a few years. Carver next became interested in trained animals, and in 1894 he added a new act, called horse diving, to his show. This involved a rider on horseback plunging off a bank and into deep water. This act was so popular that Carver ended up employing two teams of horse divers who would tour separately, and gradually he wound up his sharpshooting to concentrate entirely on trained animals.

Horse diving became Carver's lifeblood in the final decades of this life, as he outlived his great rival Buffalo Bill. In 1927 he attended a convention that was organised for all surviving ex-frontiersmen and seemed to enjoy the occasion. Following this, however, he went into a deep depression, partly brought on by the loss of his favourite horse, and died soon afterwards.

Doc Carver was entirely self-trained with guns and therefore represents an amazing natural talent. Despite this, he is often remembered for his rivalry with Buffalo Bill and his work in the entertainment industry, particularly the invention of horse diving.

John Wesley Hardin

A notorious outlaw and gunfighter, John Wesley Hardin (1853-1895) claimed to have killed over forty men. Born in Bonham, Texas, to Methodist parents, his early life involved a good deal of travel; his father roamed all over central Texas as a preacher, before settling down in 1869 in the town of Sumpter. Here he taught in a school which the younger Hardin attended.

John Hardin's first brush with trouble occurred when he was still at school, when he was attacked by another boy with a knife. Before his assailant could stab him, Hardin drew his own knife and slashed at his foe, seriously wounding and nearly killing him. A few years later he killed his first man; an ex-slave of his father's challenged him to a wrestling match and things turned nasty when Hardin won. The following day his opponent attacked him with a stick, events soon escalated and the young man ended up shooting his adversary several times, fatally wounding him. Following this he was encouraged by his father to go on the run, fearing that although a case could be made for self-defence, he would not receive a fair trial. His life as an outlaw truly began when three Union soldiers were sent to arrest him, and in a brief fire fight he shot down and killed all of them, meaning that he had slain four men while still in his mid-teens.

On Christmas Day 1869, Hardin met a man named Jim Bradley in a saloon and began playing poker against him. After an incredible run of luck saw Hardin win almost every hand, Bradley began to grow agitated and eventually threatened his opponent's life if he won another hand. Being unarmed, Hardin left quietly, but later that night the two men encountered one another again. Shots were fired and Bradley was killed. Over the next few months he slew at least two more men, after getting into arguments with them. Feeling that things were growing too hot for him to handle, he signed up with a cattle drive to Kansas.

By 1871 Hardin was back in Texas and was arrested for the murder of a city marshal, although he claimed to be innocent of this crime. While held in prison he managed to obtain a pistol and used it to escape from his captors while he was being transported in order to stand trial. He shot one guard dead and then fled, later having his shackles removed by an obliging blacksmith. Following this, his family managed to have him appointed as trail boss for a cattle drive to Abilene, but even while doing legitimate work he could not stay out of trouble. On the way the herd almost became mixed up with a Mexican drive and harsh words were exchanged between the two camps. Eventually a gunfight ensued and six Mexicans were killed.

In Abilene, Hardin encountered the marshal, Wild Bill Hickok, who forced him to hand over his guns but did not arrest him. The young man seems to have had a great respect for Hickok who was by this time quite famous for his skill with firearms. However, on a subsequent visit to Abilene, Hardin fired his guns through the ceiling of his hotel room because he was annoyed by the snoring of the guest above him. One of the shots hit the man and killed him, and Hardin fled town rather than face Wild Bill.

Unable to stay out of trouble for long, Hardin became involved in a dispute between two clans, the Taylor family and the Sutton family, in which he ended up helping to kill a local sheriff named Jack Helm. Soon afterwards, in 1872, he was seriously wounded by a shotgun blast after another dispute about gambling and almost died. Seeking to settle down to a more law-abiding life he surrendered to the authorities and asked them to charge him for his past crimes. However, on learning just how many murders they intended to charge him with, he had a change of heart and managed to escape by sawing through the bars of his cell window. Two years later Hardin was involved in the killing of a local deputy sheriff and as a result of this a lynch mob murdered his brother and two of his cousins.

Hardin's luck finally ran out after a $4,000 bounty was placed on his arrest. Several law enforcement agents boarded a train on which he was travelling and managed to capture him after a brief fight. It is said that Hardin's guns became tangled in his suspenders, meaning that he could not draw in time to defend himself. He was subsequently tried and sentenced to twenty-five years imprisonment for the murder of the deputy sheriff.

Gradually acclimatising to life in prison, Hardin read books on theology and law and tried to improve his mind as much as possible. He was eventually released in 1894, after seventeen years behind bars. Now in his early forties, he soon obtained a license to practice law and married a much younger woman, though the marriage failed almost at once for unknown reasons; following this Hardin moved to El Paso. Sadly, he could not change his ways and before long was involved in a dispute with some locals. While playing poker in a saloon he was shot in the back of the head by a man named Selman, and killed instantly.

Although some of his killings could be classed as self-defence, Hardin caused trouble wherever he went and it was really only a matter of time before he was killed. By the end of his life, as society was becoming less violent, he was still living in the past, unable to turn his life around and move into modern America.

Annie Oakley

One of the first female stars in American history, Annie Oakley (born Phoebe Ann Mosey, 1860-1926) was the finest sharpshooter of the Old West, having a professional career that spanned almost fifty years. Born in rural western Ohio to Quaker parents, Annie had a tough upbringing, losing both her natural father and then her stepfather. At the age of nine she was put into the care of the local county poor farm, where she learned basic skills such as needlework and decorating. After this she had a spell living with a local family but was treated very badly by them, later referring to them as 'the wolves'. She eventually moved back in with her family, sometime around her early teens. From a very young age Annie had taken to hunting, and to selling the game that she caught to local hotels and restaurants, thus gaining experience with firearms which was to be vital later in life.

By her early twenties, Oakley was becoming well known in the area for her skill with guns. The breakthrough came towards the start of 1861 when the Baughman and Butler shooting act came to Cincinnati. Frank Butler (1850-1926) was an Irish immigrant and earned his living as a travelling marksman. He had placed a $100 bet that he could take on and beat any local sharpshooter, and so a match was arranged against the twenty-one year old Annie. It was a close game, with both parties making virtually every shot, but eventually Frank missed and Annie was the champion. Despite losing, Butler began to court Annie, and they were married the following year. Around this time the couple took up residence in the Oakley area of Cincinnati, and Annie used this as her stage name for the rest of her life.

In 1885 they joined Buffalo Bill's Wild West Show. Another performer was the Native leader Sitting Bull, who was so impressed by the diminutive Oakley's talents that he referred to her as 'Little Sure Shot', a name which was soon being used in advertising. The only downside to her early rise to fame was an intense rivalry with another female sharpshooter, Lillian Smith. Owing to this, Annie actually left the show for a brief period but soon returned when Smith departed. Frank Butler continued to shoot, but his main role was to deal with the finances and other legal matters to do with his wife's activities. Trusting her husband with the business side of things allowed Annie to concentrate all her efforts on becoming more and more skilled with firearms.

Soon her fame had spread not just through America but throughout the entire world, and a European tour was arranged. Oakley performed in front of Queen Victoria, King Umberto of Italy, the President of France and Kaiser Wilhelm II of the new Germany. An interesting anecdote exists from this time, according to which Wilhelm asked Oakley to prove her skills by shooting the ash off the end of a cigarette that he was holding. Annie obliged and made the shot with ease. Whether or not this story is true is not certain, but it has often been said that had Annie only missed and shot the Kaiser by mistake then World War One would probably have been avoided!

Oakley believed that women should be able to serve in the armed forces, and as a result spent a great deal of time teaching many thousands of women how to shoot. She also believed that everybody, regardless of gender, should be able to use firearms as a useful means of defence, as well as a fine method of mental and physical exercise.

It seemed that Oakley's career was over in 1901 when she was involved in a train crash and damaged her spine, leaving her temporarily paralysed. Despite this, after several operations on her spine she made an almost total recovery. Perhaps as a result of this brush with death, she decided on a career change and began starring in a stage play, The Western Girl, written especially for her.

In 1903 a newspaper printed a false story claiming that Annie had been arrested for stealing in order to support a Cocaine habit. This story was widely believed and repeated in other newspapers across the country. Oakley counterattacked and over the following years won over fifty libel cases in order to restore her name.

As Annie grew older, her skills increased even more, and in her sixties she could still hit a playing card side on at ninety feet with a rifle. She was out of action for a spell after an automobile accident in 1922, but recovered to shoot again in 1924, still setting new records. Her health began to break down in 1925 and she died the following year. Frank Butler was so devastated by her death that he went into a deep depression, refused to eat and died a few weeks later.

Annie Oakley is remembered as not only the best shot of the Old West, but as probably the greatest natural shooting talent who has ever lived. Entirely self-taught, she beat all comers and only increased in skill as she aged. She also seems to have had a heart of gold; after her death it was found that she had spent almost her entire fortune on charitable gifts.

Pawnee Bill

Far less well known than Buffalo Bill, Gordon William Lillie (1860-1942) was known as Pawnee Bill because of his association with Pawnee Indians. He founded several Wild West shows, which met with varying success, and is best remembered for working with Buffalo Bill for a time.

An intelligent and resourceful man, Pawnee Bill used the railroads to great effect, moving from town to town with a rapidly changing cast as he attempted to earn a decent living with his shows. He married May Manning in 1886, and two years later they started their new production 'Pawnee Bill's Historic Wild West Indian Museum and Encampment Show'. The show was popular with audiences, but Lillie always struggled to make enough money. Performances involved Mexican bandits, Japanese actors, Pawnee Indians and Arab jugglers, making it one of the most well rounded of the various touring companies.

Towards the end of the 1800s Pawnee Bill and Buffalo Bill went into business together with the 'Two Bills' show. Despite being popular it was not a financial success and was forced to close early.

While Lillie was touring, May developed their ranch, and in later years the couple tried their hand at acting, film making and selling Indian and Mexican crafts. This operation was shut down after their home burnt to the ground in 1930. In 1936 Bill lost control of their car and May was killed. Never fully recovering from his wounds, he died in 1942, having long outlived the age which he had portrayed.

Very much in the shadow of Buffalo Bill, Gordon Lillie nevertheless managed to lead a full and exciting life, and had his part to play in the creation of the legend of the American West.

Wounded Knee Massacre

The last major action fought between the US army and Native Americans, the Wounded Knee Massacre was a tragedy which resulted in a large loss of life and effectively ended the Indian Wars. In the years leading up to the event, the government had been trying to coerce the Lakota into giving up more of their lands. The large herds of bison, along with other staples of the Sioux diet, had almost been driven to extinction; meanwhile Congress had failed to keep its treaty promises to protect reservation Indians from encroachment by settlers and gold miners. In this time of unrest, a prophet called Wovoka founded the Ghost Dance movement, based on a vision that Jesus Christ had returned to earth as a Native American. It was believed that the Messiah would return, the white man would disappear from Indian lands and all the buffalo and other animals which had been killed would be restored. The natives would then live on the earth in peace alongside their ancestors. This desirable vision attracted many, but alarmed the US military who were worried that it could spark wide-scale unrest among the Indians.

At the Standing Rock Agency, where Chief Sitting Bull lived, it was decided to take some of the native leaders into captivity in an attempt to dull the 'Messiah craze'. As police arrived to take Sitting Bull into captivity, a fight broke out which resulted in several deaths including that of the Chief, causing tensions to rise even higher. On December 28th 1890, Chief Spotted Elk of the Lakota and three hundred and fifty of his followers were intercepted by a cavalry detachment. The troops escorted the Indians to Wounded Knee Creek where they made camp for the night. In total there were around five hundred soldiers and about three hundred and fifty natives, of whom the vast majority were women and children.

The troops surrounded Spotted Elk's camp and prepared for the possibility of violence by preparing four rapid fire Hotchkiss guns. At dawn, the order was given for all natives to be disarmed and then moved onto waiting trains. What exactly happened next is unclear, but it is likely that one of the Indians refused to give up his rifle, saying that he had paid a large amount of money for it; whatever the cause, a shot was fired and suddenly a huge fire-fight began. Many of the casualties occurred in the first moments of the battle as the government forces fired on their largely unarmed opponents. The Hotchkiss guns were turned against the women and children, forcing them to run for cover, seeking shelter from the crossfire in a nearby ravine. Many of the army casualties were probably caused by friendly fire in the confused fighting; in all the conflict lasted well under an hour, with one hundred and fifty Lakota dead against twenty-five soldiers.

There was a minor action the following day, but Wounded Knee was basically the end of the centuries-long Indian Wars, and represented a good deal of the mutual misunderstanding and simmering hatred that existed between natives and whites. It is a real human tragedy that could so easily have been avoided had it been better handled. Decades later Black Elk, an eye witness to the battle, summed it up in these words:

"I did not know then how much was ended. When I look back now from this high hill of my old age, I can still see the butchered women and children lying heaped and scattered all along the crooked gulch as plain as when I saw them with eyes young. And I can see that something else died there in the bloody mud, and was buried in the blizzard. A people's dream died there. It was a beautiful dream."

The Dalton Gang

Interestingly enough, the Dalton family involved both lawmen and outlaws. The gang specialised in bank and train robberies during a brief period at the beginning of the 1890s, and were relatives of the Younger brothers who were involved with Jesse James and his group of bandits. Growing up in Jackson County, Missouri, the family eventually moved to Oklahoma in what was at the time known as Indian Territory. By 1886 they had moved again, this time to Coffeyville in south-east Kansas, settling down to a life of farming. However, the railroad which was built in the area ruined the family farm and may have set the brothers on the road to crime.

One son, Frank, was a deputy US Marshal and was killed in the line of duty in 1887, while tracking a horse thief. In the ensuing shootout several men were slain including Frank. This had the effect of further unsettling his brothers, as he had always been a well-respected and stabilising influence on them. The three younger Dalton boys, Grat, Bob and Emmett, became lawmen themselves; however, in 1890 they turned to crime after not being paid on several occasions. Apparently Bob was the wildest of the three and had already killed a man by the time he was nineteen, though this was while he was a Deputy Marshal, and he claimed that it was done in the line of duty. After a few narrow escapes from the law for several offences, such as horse stealing and illegal liquor trading, the boys formed their first gang.

Taking the lead, Bob recruited several more members to ride with them, and their first raid was on a gambling house in New Mexico. On February 6th 1891, after the gang had been joined by another brother called Jack, a train was held up and the Daltons were accused of the robbery, even though there was little evidence linking them to it. Jack escaped but Grat was arrested, found guilty and given a twenty-year prison sentence. While being transferred by train, accompanied by two deputies, one of whom was handcuffed to him, he made a daring escape. Somehow he got hold of the key to the handcuffs and undid them while the deputy slept. He then leapt out of the train window as it was going over a bridge, landing in the water and being carried away by the current. He survived the ordeal and soon joined up with his brothers once again.

Over the next year the gang held up several trains and also dabbled in other crimes such as horse theft. In 1892 they robbed a train of $10,000 and escaped with their loot. They tended to rob passengers as well as going for the safe, though quite often they would fail to steal much that was valuable and so it was rather a hit and miss affair. In July they made an audacious robbery in which they arrived at a train station and robbed it, before waiting for the train to arrive and then holding it up. On this occasion there were armed guards on the train and a gunfight ensued in which a bystander was shot and killed. Following this, the gang hid out in local caves.

Despite their success with trains, Bob Dalton wanted their name to go down in history and was worried that other outlaws, such as Jesse James, were more famous than he was. As a result of this he decided that they should attempt to rob two banks at once, and to do so in broad daylight. To achieve this they returned to Coffeyville in Kansas, wearing false beards in an attempt to stop local people from recognising them. Despite this precaution they were quickly identified and while the gang attempted to rob the banks, the local people armed themselves and prepared for a gun battle. As soon as the men came out of the bank, shots were fired and the situation quickly became a desperate fire fight. The local Marshal was hit and slain, but still managed to gun down one member of the gang as he died. Grat and Bob Dalton and two other members of the gang were killed. Emmett Dalton received twenty-three gunshot wounds but somehow survived and was taken into custody.

Coffeyville spelt the end of the Dalton gang, though Emmett was pardoned after serving fourteen years in prison. He moved to Kansas and lived until 1937, working as a real estate agent, author and actor. Utterly renouncing his criminal past he died at the age of sixty-six.

In his attempt at becoming just as famous as Jesse James, it has to be said that Bob Dalton failed. He did, however, make a name for himself at the time, and managed to earn an enduring legacy. The gang was essentially a violent product of violent times, but was already something of an anachronism, coming close to the end of the Old West.

Conclusion

The story goes that there was once a traveller in the American West who found himself chased by hostile Indians. Having taken shelter in a cave he was eventually forced by lack of water to go outside and face his pursuers. Despite being outnumbered six to one, he had a secret weapon which was one of the new revolvers, capable to firing many shots without reloading. As the Indians attacked he fired three shots in quick succession, slaying three of his opponents and causing the others to flee. The man was quick to offer a prayer of thanks for Samuel Colt and the others who had been involved in the development of firearms.

In many ways the history of the Old West is the history of the gun. From the Winchester Repeating Rifle to the Colt Peacemaker, the advances in firearm technology that took place in the nineteenth-century redefined the frontier and finally gave the US the decisive advantage over the natives. In particular the horrors of the Civil War caused a new generation to grow up who were used to the ways of violence, and it is no coincidence that the final few decades before the modern era tended to see the most colourful characters, heroic lawmen and desperate outlaws.

Our view of the period today is greatly coloured by film, television and books, which have presented their own version of the 'Wild West', some of which is based on truth and some little more than fantasy. However, back in the nineteenth century men like Buffalo Bill were creating the myth even as they were living it, and stories of frontier life were very popular long before the advent of the cinema. People such as Jesse James, who saw his crimes as part profit-making and part publicity stunt, were also adding to the legend, quite aware of the effect that their actions were having on the popular mindset; there is simply no other period in history that is so rife with its own mythology.

The story of the West is also, in one sense, a story of tragedy, as the Native Americans were gradually pushed out of their lands and forced onto reservations. Ever since the first Europeans arrived there had been tensions, and the Indian Wars went on for centuries. The ways of life of the Natives and the Whites were just too different, too incompatible, for them to have ever lived together in peace. The massacre at Wounded Knee was the final major action in this drama, and in some ways sums the whole thing up; the total inability of the two sides to work out their differences and the utter lack of trust were a true recipe for disaster.

For all its highs and lows, the time of the Old West remains etched into modern thinking; there is something about the rugged terrain, the gunfights and the frontier spirit which appeals to the twenty-first century mind, drawing us back again and again into another world.